FIVESTARMAN
THE FIVE PASSIONS OF AUTHENTIC MANHOOD

Neil Kennedy

MY HEALTHY CHURCH
www.MyHealthyChurch.com

Published by My Healthy Church
1445 N. Boonville Ave., Springfield, MO 65802.

In instances where no reference is given, the Scripture quotation is taken from the King James Version of the Bible. Public domain.

Unless otherwise indicated, all Scripture quotations with references are taken from The Holy Bible, New International Version®. NIV®. Copyright © 1973, 1978, 1984 by Biblica, Inc.™ Used by permission. All rights reserved worldwide. The "NIV" and "New International Version" are trademarks registered in the United States Patent and Trademark Office by Biblica, Inc.™

Scripture quotations marked NLT are taken from The Holy Bible: New Living Translation, copyright © 2004 by Tyndale Charitable Trust. Used by permission of Tyndale House Publishers, Carol Stream, Illinois.

ISBN: 978-1-62423-054-7

Printed in the United States of America

16 15 14 13 . 2 3 4 5 6

For men who are willing to rise up and
resurrect authentic manhood.

CONTENTS

PASSION FIVE
PHILANTHROPIC CAUSE

CONCLUSION
THE CHALLENGE

INTRODUCTION

He half stumbles along the sidewalk as he walks, a cigarette clinging to his lips, beneath his unkempt, straggly beard. His eyebrows and hair are sporadic weeds. His leathered skin, accented by crevasses and age spots, cover his weakened body. His clothes are as unkempt as his attitude. His eyes are yellowed and bloodshot. He burps out curses from his odorous mouth. His belly protrudes out from his midsection, exposed by the shirt that has either shrunk or, long ago, outlived its coverage. His condition proclaims to the world his regret, *If I'd known I would live this long, I would have taken better care of mysel.*

This guy represents millions of men who have decided that they will live the "eat-drink-for-tomorrow-we-die" lifestyle. They have their own theme songs, clothing lines, and their, *"I don't give a *#%!"* attitudes.

Man doesn't start out to live this way. He embarks in life with dreams and ambitions, but somewhere along the way in the daily grind, the resistance causes his dreams to become faded memories. By the time he hits forty, he no longer looks at the stars as lofty goals yet to be reached; they become faded wishes, leading him to wonder how much longer he will toil under them. Awake at night, restless, zoned-out, his fitful routine makes him all the more tired of just existing.

His wife is equally tired from the workload of the house. The bills pile up on the desk, awaiting their turn. She weeps at night, lonely, confused, and sad. Her prince has surrendered. He no longer rescues her from evil. He no longer whisks her up into his arms. He abandons her to the bedroom. The romance of young love has died. His love is as impotent as his sex drive.

His children are raised in the insecurity of a leaderless home. Their instructions for life come not from a father directing their paths but from peers who have adopted the ways of stupidity. The children's heroes are fantasies, man-made idols from Hollywood, who live the glamorous life of cars, clothes, cocaine, and cottages. They're famous for . . . nothing really, but they're famous. Drugs become a way of escape, a way to dull the feelings of absent love. Their teens become so frustrated yet can't be heard, so they mutilate and tattoo their bodies in a desperate attempt to get attention. They cry out, *"Please notice me, correct me, help me . . . I'm scared."*

The thrill of life is dulled by routine.

Most men can't put their finger on the moment, the exact time and place when they decided to lay down their dreams. Most men can't tell you when their authentic manhood was surrendered. They just gradually give up and proclaim, *"If I had known I would live this long, I would have taken better care of myself. I would have done things differently."*

AUTHENTIC MAN

Are you an authentic man?

Really?

When did that happen? When did you decide that you were a man? Who told you, and who gave you the rite of passage to manhood?

Many cultures have clearly defined rites of passage to manhood. A ritual is observed—a celebration with the community, a mark on the forehead, or the fulfillment of a challenge confirms him.

In Western culture when a boy becomes a man, we mark small rites, such as when a boy gets a driver's license, is eligible for the military, or is old enough to purchase alcohol, but we do not have spiritual rites of passage into manhood. Marriage is considered by some to be the closest recognition of movement into manhood. The definition of manhood in our time is confused. When do we recognize a male as a man?

Our sons step into manhood without fanfare or celebration. We don't define it. We don't have set principles that govern what authentic manhood is.

"WHEN THE PURPOSE IS UNKNOWN, ABUSE IS INEVITABLE."
—DR. MYLES MONROE

We are witnessing the inevitable abuse of manhood. The last forty years has wreaked havoc on authentic manhood. The feminization of men is displayed in a constant barrage of media imagery. Almost every male represented on television is either a metro-sexual pretty boy or a slovenly buffoon. Every reality show has to have its token effeminate male. It's embarrassing.

This assault on authentic masculinity has a very broad impact. I won't go through the barrage of statistics that support my claims; suffice it to say that the destruction of authentic manhood is having enormous repercussions on society. Some subcultures are already reeling from the loss of authentic man. Fatherless children are being raised with the insecurities that come from the loss of identity. Women are being left defenseless against the enmity that exists against them. The economic decline caused by the loss of male integrity is immeasurable.

"NEVER REMOVE A FENCE UNTIL YOU KNOW WHY IT WAS PUT UP."
—UNKNOWN

Boundaries are important. The foundation of manhood is being redefined. Unless we know why the male is a man, or what man is assigned to do or become, we will live abusive lives. We may abuse our own bodies with addictions such as alcohol, drugs, or food. We may abuse ourselves sexually and experience the degradation of our bodies through STDs or AIDS. The frustrations of unknown purpose may cause us to abuse our wives and misunderstand the true value of the male/female relationship.

"FOR EVERY MILE OF ROAD THERE ARE TWO MILES OF DITCH."
—ANONYMOUS

Extremes take over. We will either become obsessive chauvinists or emasculated weaklings.

But to discover purpose, you simply need to look at original intent. Why did God create man?

The identity of authentic manhood runs deep within us. *"The purposes of a man are deep rivers, the man who understands this draws upon them"* (Proverbs 20:5, author's paraphrase).

Within every man are purposes and passions that are uniquely male, yet we are being told that there is nothing inherently special or purposeful about manhood. Women, liberated from dominated positions, have increasingly taken a lead role in society. By September 2010, there were more women employed than there were men. Touting this fact, the cover of the *Atlantic Journal* headlined this bold title, "THE END OF MEN."

Don't get me wrong, I don't blame women for stepping up to exercise their liberty from oppressive or ignorant men who have abused them, or from lazy men who have not provided for them; however, radical feminism has violently attacked any semblance of a man's uniqueness, rather than embracing their own special feminine identity.

Some men have surrendered their roles and special assignments, even taking on the mannerisms and roles of a female.

My friend, George Sawyer proclaimed, "Just as Lazarus laid in the tomb until Jesus called him by name, it is time to hear that Voice for the resurrection of manhood, to step out of the tomb, to unwrap ourselves from the bandages of decay, and proclaim that we are alive!"

This book is a proclamation to call man out of his grave clothes and walk again in a resurrected life. The truths in this book are not just to be read through quickly, but they are to be processed. I don't intend to just argue out the case, but to inspire you to reclaim authentic manhood. I want to speak to the issue, but more importantly, to challenge every male that I can to dig deep into himself to discover and understand the passions of authentic manhood.

The purposes of a man are deep rivers. There are currents that flow in the DNA of every man of who he is and what he is purposed to be. The Five Passions will not only impart something to you, but they will draw something out of you. As you are reading this book, be ready to change your posture, your attitude, and your life, and get ready to become the authentic man that God created you to be.

IDENTITY LOST

I can't remember very much of my early childhood. There are faded glimpses of memories, a picture of playing near a stream in the back of the house trying to catch tadpoles, playing football in the field across the street, falling asleep in the barber's chair, stubbornly refusing to eat peas because my hypersensitive sense of smell repulsed at their pungent odor.

One memory stands out with vivid clarity. It was the moment that my mother called my brother, my sister, and me into her room so that we could talk to our father on the phone. My father traveled a lot in his position as a purchasing agent for General Electric. We would talk on the phone occasionally; however, this call was different. The look on my mother's face was pity and sadness. I knew something was wrong.

My older brother took the phone, and within seconds he burst into tears. I couldn't imagine what was happening. My sister was next to put her ear to the phone. Tears began to silently drip down her face. I remember seeing her eyes glaze over, as if she were in a fog.

Then it was my turn.

As I took the phone, my father's deep baritone voice spoke matter of factly. "Son, your mother and I are not going to be married any longer. I won't be living at home. I love you little buddy."

I can't remember any more. At five years of age, I couldn't grasp what this would mean to me or how it would define me.

The next few years are a blur. The time frame is baffling. My mother began to date a man who was once a business associate of my father's. Obviously, I was too young to understand the dynamics of adultery, only to find out some of the distorted details later in life. For a child, everything was out of sync. It was as if the rhythm of my life had been interrupted. I would spend my childhood seemingly out of step with everyone, confused and dazed by the whole thing.

One instance seems to define my childhood experience. My mother had been to the grocery store. She treated us with single-pack Reese's Peanut Butter Cups. I knew that Reese's normally come two to a package, so after I enjoyed one cup, I asked for another. The strange man firmly interrupted my mother's "Yes" with a harsh tone and said, "No." He intimidated my mother, and she agreed with him. I didn't get to eat the second Reese's.

I was confused. Who was this guy? Who was he to determine my diet?

My mother married him. He was a strange man, but all of a sudden, he was supposed to be my father. I couldn't understand that.

He forced my mother to stop calling me by my given name, "Gary," and started referring to me as "Neil," which is my middle name. Then he dropped my name "Kennedy," and gave me "Roberson" as my last name. In one swift move, my identity was lost.

Every school year on the first day of class, my new teacher would call roll. "Gary Kennedy." I remember the embarrassment of walking to the teacher's desk each September to explain the stupidity of my life.

This identity theft impacted me more than you can imagine. My thoughts were constantly, *Who are you?*

I had no heritage. I had no baseline. I had no father to tell me of his past and direct my future.

This confusion was only exacerbated by the constant strife in our home. Alcohol abuse, occasional physical abuse, and daily (if not hourly) verbal assaults were the norm.

My biological father remarried and focused his attention on raising his new wife's five children. I saw him only a few times during my childhood and on two occasions as a teen. My mother and grandparents implied that I was disloyal to my mother if I showed any admiration or love toward my real father.

I have rarely talked about this part of my life, but it serves as a metaphor for how a boy can struggle with his identity to become an authentic man. I am only one of millions of boys who have a similar story or even worse family dysfunctions.

> ## "IT IS INSANITY TO DO THE SAME THING REPEATEDLY AND EXPECT DIFFERENT RESULTS."
> —ALBERT EINSTEIN

Somehow I inherently knew that all of my training was wrong. I knew deep within me that I would have the same life that I'd seen modeled before me, unless I did something different.

ORIGINAL INTENT

We are doomed to repeat the failed patterns of life if we do not discover the truths of authentic manhood. Insecurities will overwhelm us if we do not gain the confidence that comes from purpose. To become an authentic man means that we need to find the original intent of manhood.

First of all, we must have the foundational belief that we were created with the Intelligent Design of purpose. Without a Creator, we are meaningless; our existence is flatulence in the wind.

If man is designed and purposed by a Creator, then the Creator defines him. We must start at the beginning to discover His original intent for man. Anything less is the ultimate arrogance.

How can the creation mockingly respond to the Creator, "Why did you make me this way?"

"Let us make man...."

After the formation of Earth and the gathering of waters, dry land appeared. Before God released the agrarian system of provision, He designed the purpose of the Earth. The Psalmist said, *"The Earth was made for man."*

God used clay to mold, fashion, and frame the shadow of His image into a piece of living art. Then He breathed into man's nostrils the element of life. Man became a living being.

The very first statement that God spoke over man gives us insight into His original intent, *"Be fruitful and increase."*

Within your genetic code is the drive to succeed and increase. Within you is the purpose of reproduction. Within you is the increasing desire to grow your numbers. As Solomon said, *"No man is ever satisfied with his income."* It is diametrically opposed to the original intent of man not to want increase, numerically or economically.

It's not greed to desire increase; it's God's original intent. Greed is born out of covetousness, which is the desire to have another man's possessions at his expense. Greed is born out of a narcissistic attitude that fails to understand God's provision.

The flaw in covetous thinking is the basic economic theory that my gain comes at the expense of another person. Modern economics is built upon the idea that the pie is only so big for a few elites to eat of it. Society does not trust the God of Creation to be wise enough to deposit within the Earth enough resources to sustain and prosper all people.

Solomon said, *"As goods increase, so do consumers" (Ecclesiastes 5:11, author's paraphrase).*

God repeatedly declares over man His intent to populate the earth. Yet, if you listen to the arguments of the fringe, they espouse controlling the increase of man, claiming that we are overpopulating the Earth. Their idea is that man is inherently bad for the Earth. Abortion becomes a sadistic means of controlling populations, just as euthanasia will soon be an acceptable means to serve their purpose. Abortion is called, "choice." Euthanasia will be called, "mercy."

It is always interesting to see the hypocrisy of the living argue against more people "living." They love only themselves. If they really believed that mankind was bad for the Earth, they could easily eliminate at least part of the problem. Their argument is silly. Claiming to be wise, they are fools.

Man is the economy.

You can't have economic increase without the increase of man himself. No country in history ever increased it's economy while simultaneously decreasing in population.

The argument against man begins with population control, which is in direct opposition to God's original intent.

The second argument is closely related, suggesting that man is the cause of "global warming," or now, since pseudo-science fraudulently "cooked the books" (pun intended), the proposed argument is "global disruption."

The claim that man is destroying the Earth is another attempt to control the increase of man economically. The claims that we are using up the resources of Earth are simply out of step with the evidence.

God's original intent for man was to *dominate* the Earth, which means we are to steward and care for the Earth. I believe that we must properly manage our cultivation of the Earth. We should develop and manage our resources with wisdom and responsibility; however, we must continue to draw upon those resources for our use and for the expansion of mankind. The resources of Earth are placed on deposit for our use and increase.

God is wise enough to create the world in which we live with more than enough to sustain, and even prosper, mankind throughout our existence.

Work is an original intent of man.

"The LORD God took the man and put him in the Garden of Eden to work it and take care of it" (Genesis 2:15). Work is not part of the curse. Quite the opposite; it is man's vocation. *Vocation* means *divine spoken word* and suggests an invitation to a feast. You are invited by the Creator to partake of ample supply when you fulfill His original intent through work.

> *A man who does not work should not eat (2 Thessalonians 3:10, author's paraphrase).*

God created work for man to fulfill purpose. Just as God worked and rested, He created man to have the rhythm of work and rest.

During the creation, God continued to stamp His work with the words, *"He saw that it was good"*—that is, until God saw man's lack. Then He pronounced, *"It is not good that man is alone."*

If man fulfills his purpose to work, then he is qualified for his next purpose: woman.

Man needed a "help-mate," someone with whom to companion, to partner, to work alongside, and to propagate mankind. God paraded the animals in front of the man for a survey. Although naming the animals, man did not find a suitable helper; nor did God make another man to be his companion.

God drew out of man his equal companion. Man is designed to be cultivated and to be a cultivator. The word *husband* means *one who cultivates*. The primary role of a husband to a wife is cultivation. It is the root of the male/female relationship. Male sows the seed of life; female receives the seed and incubates the seed until male reaps the harvest of her womb.

In a similar manner, the male is to speak words over his wife. She is to receive his words, mixing them with faith, and produce the fruit of his cultivation.

The authentic man recognizes his wife's strengths and celebrates her ability to supplement his weaknesses. God made woman his helpmate. Men and women have perfectly complementary designs.

Solomon said, *"I went past the field of the sluggard, past the vineyard of the man who lacks judgment; thorns had come up everywhere, the ground was covered with weeds, and the stone wall was in ruins"* (Proverbs 24:30–31).

Husband, after a season of time, if you do not like what your wife looks like or what she is producing, it's your fault, not hers. You need to tend to your own garden better.

Most men are slothful when it comes to cultivating their wives. When you're out in public, you can see the lack of attention that many women receive from their cultivators. They look undone, unkempt, sloppy, and disheveled, women who reflect their husband's work.

I know that some will take an offense at this responsibility. Some men will push back on it and blame the woman. Yes, some women have a Jezebel attitude or spirit. (*Jezebel* means *without cohabitation.*) Even though they are married, they will not submit to their husbands' leadership. Even so, the responsibility to lead his wife is given to man. Adam was held responsible for not leading his wife. He was the one who heard God say, *"You are not to eat of this particular tree."* It was Adam's responsibility to instruct his wife in what God had said and to give her faith to follow him by teaching her the Word of God. She was susceptible to deception because of Adam's failed leadership. Adam was not deceived. He willingly disobeyed the Word of God.

Of course, Adam not only threw his wife under the bus, but he also went so far as to blame God by saying, *"It was the woman that You gave me."* Don't be so quick to blame your lack of husbandry on your wife, and especially don't blame it on God.

Original intent is foundational to understanding who you are and what you are to do as an authentic man. When you believe in Intelligent Design rather than evolutionary chance you come away with purpose.

There are rivers that flow within you, passions relating to the original purposes that are inherent to authentic manhood. I have identified five such passions in this book:

- an *Adventurous* spirit,
- the *Entrepreneurial* drive,
- *Gallant* in relationships,
- *Faithfulness* of character, and
- *Philanthropic* in cause.

Now that we know God's original intent, it is time that we take responsibility and MAN UP!

PASSION ONE

AN ADVENTUROUS SPIRIT

PROLOGUE

Jimmy, or JJ, as most people called him, grew up playing football, wrestling, and doing just about anything else physical that he could find to do. The only magnet to bring him his father's attention was during a game, and only if he was starting. That made JJ work harder than others. It motivated him to press the weights, run the extra mile, and spend a few more minutes in the gym. His coaches loved his dedication. They knew that something other than normal competitiveness was driving his ambition, but they dared not disturb it. JJ's skills were much too valuable to mess with. They were accustomed to using JJ for their own advantage. He won games. JJ's anger, his hostility toward his opponents, bordered on rage, but it worked. He racked up the awards, all-district, all-state; his name was mentioned in scouting trips and local media. That was until the injury.

It wouldn't have made much difference in the long run, but it could have been a better story. The play that dismantled his dreams wasn't important, nor did it happen in a game of any significance. It wasn't the championship, or the playoffs. No, it wasn't even a conference game. It was a scrimmage, a pre-season match against a less-than-average opponent. The players were at half speed, just going through the motions, awaiting the Friday night lights of the fall. JJ ran over to make a tackle, when a small, ruddy fullback came out of nowhere, spearing into JJ like he was a rag doll. The impact buckled his body into a limp and mangled mess on the ground. JJ's eyes rolled back into his head and JJ entered into a dream state that bordered between fog and reality.

JJ's injury would not just move him from the starting lineup, but beyond the bench and into the stands. A mighty competitor was removed from the field of contest.

What was he going to do now? How would he be defined? How would he get the attention that he desperately craved?

Within weeks, JJ was no longer the star athlete with the promised destiny. Now, JJ was a has-been, even before his senior graduation. Those who witnessed his rise to stardom soon forgot about it. Other players became the talk of the hallway. Scouts no longer knew who JJ was; his was a vague and forgotten story.

Although he recovered from the injury, its effect on his life lingered. JJ's emotional temperament no longer had an outlet on the field. His anger boiled underneath the surface of his demeanor only to erupt on the occasions that turned embarrassing and sad. People still liked him, but something simmered beneath the surface that was so abrasive it caused them to keep their distance.

JJ assumed that every person he met was measuring him up, thinking that he was the has-been with unfulfilled potential.

To ease the pain, he picked up a couple of bad habits; smoking was a natural sedative that he adopted from his mother and father. Drinking beer was as normal as iced tea. Even though he could still wear the gear, workouts became a memory. His well-conditioned and chiseled body reshaped itself into a puffy semblance of its former glory.

Years went by. JJ lived an average life, which could have even been considered respectable by most. He married a girl who still thought of him as the all-star player. He let her think it, although he knew better. He knew he wasn't the man he was supposed to become.

Weekdays were filled with work, weeknights were bored routines, and Saturdays were reserved for yard work and seasonal sports.

It was another ordinary moment, on a less-than-average day that impacted JJ just like the injury twelve years earlier.

It wasn't at one of the church services he routinely attended to keep up appearances. It wasn't while watching the guru on television spinning his success tapes on "fire-walking" and unlimited potential. There were no alarms about his health. It was just another boring evening in his mundane life.

His children were young toddlers playing in the other room. His wife was in the kitchen cleaning up the normal spillage of crumbs that fell from the plates of children learning to eat.

It was but a whispering thought that somehow tangled itself up into his thinking. He heard a small echo within him that said, "Get your fight back."

JJ cocked his head to the side to listen.

"Get your fight back."

He turned to see if somehow his wife was speaking the coded message. She wasn't. She was too busy. The kids were not paying any attention to anything other than their own playtime fantasies.

But he heard a voice—a still, small voice, deep within him, rising up, wanting to scream out, *"Get your fight back!"* He wanted to stand up, shout it, repeat it, have a fit, dance, move, run, and express it.

He ran to the backroom, looked into the mirror with the intensity of years of pressurized anger. Then he burst into a loud voice, making eye contact with himself, and he yelled, "GET YOUR FIGHT BACK!"

AN ADVENTUROUS SPIRIT

Within every man is a spirit of adventure.

You were made out of the dirt, molded from the clay, and that's also where you are called to return. It's where you relate—the field of contest—whether it's a football field, a baseball field, a golf course, or even a battlefield. It's on the field of contest that man clashes with other men sharpening his skills and strengthening his resolve.

Women relate face-to-face sharing feelings; men relate shoulder-to-shoulder facing challenges. A woman tells you what she feels; a man tells you what he thinks.

The Bible says, *"Iron sharpens iron, a man sharpens another man" (Proverbs 27:17, author's paraphrase).* Iron does not sharpen with a caress but with a clash. You become a better man by the competition. The struggle strengthens you.

Do you always win?

No, but you become a better man. The competition conditions you.

I enjoy the game of golf. I don't like playing a hackers field. I like the ambiance of the game, the manicured landscape, and the gentlemen's rules. I like playing with men who compete without being obnoxious. Some men talk trash; others prove their skill by bringing their "A" game. The competition makes me a better golfer. When I'm playing with "D" players, I normally don't play my best, but when I play with "A" players, I play better. I play up to the challenge. I want to beat you when you play your best game.

The field of contest has always been in the heart of a man. Early man left the home to hunt in the field, to kill a wild beast, and to bring it home as a prize for his family. The family celebrated his victory by cooking and feasting on his conquest. At dinner, he was served first, because he was "The Man!"

Even though we still leave the house to enter the field of contest and return with provisions, something seems lost in translation when all we bring home is a paycheck. The family doesn't celebrate dad's victories anymore. Celebration has become expectation. The family feels cheated if the money isn't there when they want the latest cultural phenomenon. The husband/father no longer receives honor for being the provider. The dignity of vocation no longer commands respect.

> ## "ADVENTURE, WITH ALL ITS REQUISITE DANGER AND WILDNESS, IS A DEEPLY SPIRITUAL LONGING WRITTEN INTO THE SOUL OF MAN."
> —JOHN ELDREDGE

The adventurous spirit slowly dies when a man has to live his whole life refined in designer clothes. Sometimes a man needs to get back out into the dirt and play as he did when he was a child.

Some men were not even raised to get dirty. The mantra of their mothers was, "Boys— Don't get dirty!" These boys are raised in the home, around the sewing and the cooking to become effeminate, taking on the nature of a woman. When Mom is in control, the only adventure they have is playing G-rated video games.

My wife is a Southern belle. She is a precious woman with the cultural DNA of the South deeply embedded into her. When my son, Chase, was an infant and toddler, she "smocked" his clothing (an artistic design on the front of an outfit). One day Kay was dressing Chase with one of her masterful creations and attempting to put a new pair of white shoes on his feet when he started kicking and screaming, "Me don't wear girl shoes!"

That's my boy. That moment was the beginning of his pulling away from the maternal bonding that a mother and son have at birth.

THE TWINS OF CONTENTION

The biblical account of Isaac and Rebekah demonstrates the contention between the two natures of man. They had twin boys who wrestled within Rebekah's womb, causing her to have horrific pains in her pregnancy. She sought God for an answer to what was happening within her.

God answered by saying, *"Two nations are in your womb, and two peoples from within you will be separated; one people will be stronger than the other, and the older will serve the younger"* (Genesis 25:23).

God spoke to the generations within her, prophesying their future. When it came time for their birth, the twins were in contention. The first child to arrive was covered with red hair, so they named him *Esau*, which means *Red*. Grasping the heel of Red was *Jacob*, which means to *grasp the heel*, or figuratively means *to deceive*.

Red was loved by his father. He learned to be a skillful hunter, a man who liked to be out in the field. He was loud, and rough-hewn.

Red wasn't a thinker. He didn't have vision beyond his present appetite. This exposed a weakness, his vulnerability to be deceived.

Rebekah loved Deceiver. She schooled his quiet nature, kept him around the tents, dressed him in designer clothes, and taught him how to cook. She also taught him the subtle techniques of deception.

Red came home from a failed day of hunting, when Deceiver welcomed him with a contract, "Will you trade a fresh bowl of stew for your birthright?"

Red's stomach controlled his passion, so he made hasty decisions. *"Haste leads to poverty" (Proverbs 21:5).* Deceiver's passion was his legacy; he would strive for significance, even if he achieved it through evil means.

This war between the natures of man continues to jostle back and forth. You may have the two natures within you. You may immediately identify with Red, or you may realize that you have a secret nature that relates to Deceiver.

This imbalance can stem from how we raise our children. When a parent favors a child, they want to put their imprint upon that child. Isaac related to Esau, while Rebekah was devoted to Jacob. Even though they were raised in the same household, they were parented separately, as if they were each living in a single-parent household.

We can see the devastating effects of single-parent households every day. I can't tell you how many horrific stories I've heard, where a fatherless boy is manipulated into deception by a predator because the boy needed a "daddy" in his life. Boys crave the love of a father.

We need the balance of both natures. We need to be in the field, hunting, fishing, hiking, riding, exploring and adventuring, and we need to be thinking long term, so that our temporary appetites don't forfeit our futures.

GOD WRESTLES WITH MAN ALONE

Growing up in Oklahoma, my sport of choice was wrestling. I was fortunate to have a very good coach; one who conditioned us physically, instructed us on the strategies of a match, and also mentored us in life. He taught us how to conduct ourselves before, during, and after a match. It was required of us to wear sport coats and ties to tournaments. This was old school, but it worked. Somehow it gave us a mental edge over our opponents. I was so proud to be a part of the wrestling team. It gave me a source of identity at a young and impressionable age.

We trained hard. In the miserably cold winter, we would turn the gas heater up and rig it so it would not turn off. We wore multiple layers of sweats to train. We punished our bodies beyond what modern wisdom would recommend, until one day, one of our teammates became sick. Pneumonia set in and he died.

Our beloved coach resigned. He left coaching. He left the school. He faded away into obscurity, hiding behind the shame of blame. The team never recovered.

Everything changed that year. We couldn't get our fight back.

"So Jacob was left alone, and a man wrestled with him till daybreak" (Genesis 32:24).

You are alone and wrestling with God. God deals with man . . . alone. It is in the moments of isolation where you will find your fight. God won't deal with you in a group setting. He doesn't address the fraternity, the team, the union, or societies; ***God wrestles one on one.***

This is when you shake off your vanity and ideologies and get down into the grasp of Someone stronger and more powerful than you ever dreamed.

When I was a young man, I found myself in a unique station in life. I had a beautiful wife, three young children, cars, clothes, and a cottage. I had reached a level of success that surprised me. And I was so . . . depressed.

There was no reason for it. The spirit of depression surrounded me. It haunted me at night. It was more than just having a bad day—it was a constant cloud of darkness.

One night as I tossed and turned, I finally went outside, crawled into a hammock, and looking up into the sky, I prayed, "God can you please do something to help me?" I craved the soothing caress of a loving Father. But I got a surprise. God spoke to me saying, "Neil, get up!"

Proverbs says, *"Wounds from a friend can be trusted"* (27:6). God wrestled with me. Pushed me. Challenged me. He fought with me that night. Every move I tried on Him, He countered with a more strategic blow. It was simply awesome. I found myself intimate with God by wrestling with Him. I discovered His blessing that night. We became close.

Jacob said, *"I will not let you go unless you bless me"* (Genesis 32:26).

THE PASTURE OF PREPARATION

Every boy sees a field differently. Some see a place to hunt. Some see a place to ride motocross. Some see a place to hit or throw a ball. Every man knows that the game is a metaphor for life. The rules are there to manage the chaos of the competition. Learning the game, whatever the game may be, prepares a boy for manhood.

David was born the eighth child of Jesse. He was a small and ruddy guy, good looking, loyal, and truthful in his manners. David shepherded his father's sheep. He was in the pasture many times alone, isolated, left to ponder the stars, and wander the woods.

Isolation is a unique experience.

I learned the value of isolation when I was hired shortly after my high school graduation to pump water out of an open pit in a coal mine. I went to work at 7:00 p.m. and worked through the night until 7:00 a.m. I was completely alone. Today the company would face hefty fines for working me that way, but at the time, my desperation to work outweighed the fears of the job.

Solomon said, *"The laborer's appetite works for him; his hunger drives him on"* (Proverbs 16:26).

I spent a full year without missing one night of work. I was young, naïve, and hungry—very hungry. To be honest, those nights were the conditioning of my life. That coal mine became my pasture of preparation.

Most of my dreams were conceived during those nights of isolation. Many of the things I've seen come to pass in life can be traced to embracing the challenge of being left out in the field to ponder the sky, to consider my purpose, to question my life.

David proved himself in the pasture of preparation. When a lion came to devour the flock, David sprang into action to rescue the lamb. (The zeal of youth is expressed more by adrenaline than by wisdom.) David's loyalty for his father's possessions seemed more valuable than his own life. When a bear attacked the herd, David rose up against it. The isolation drew out his authentic manhood.

There comes a time in a boy's life when he must be willing to risk it all.

One night in the coal mine, I was faced with a very difficult decision. It was a bitterly cold night. The mine had been shut down for a couple of years due to a strike. Water filled the strip mine up at least fifty feet deep. It was my responsibility to maintain the water pumps while they worked against the constant flow of underground streams.

In order to get to the water pump, I had to maneuver a small boat to a barge where the pump was stationed. The water had frozen over. I had to break the ice to get there. It was exhausting work. Underneath my coveralls, I was sweating, even though the temperature was well below zero degrees.

My frustration of remaining in the boat with little or no progress caused me to step out onto the ice and begin to drag the boat behind me to the pump. I was finally making progress, when all of a sudden the ice began to crack. Within seconds, I had fallen through. Somehow I was able to stabilize the boat and get back into it. My next decision wasn't any wiser than the first. I decided that I would go ahead and check the pump before I returned to the heater in my truck. When I finally returned I was frozen. I can't tell you how miserable that experience was, but it taught me some valuable lessons.

- **ISOLATION IS INTIMIDATING**
  It is a place where you discover vulnerabilities. It can expose your weaknesses.
- **ISOLATION IS QUIET**
  You begin to hear your spirit as loud as the sounds of a city in the middle of the day.
- **ISOLATION IS REVEALING**
  You begin to realize there is activity all around you that is happening in the dark.
- **ISOLATION EXPANDS YOU**
  When people constantly surround you, you begin to place yourself within acceptable limits. When you stand under the stars, the outer-limits become accessible. You begin to dream beyond the boundaries of others.
- **ISOLATION TESTS YOUR CHARACTER**
  When no one can see you, you become who you really are.

"Obey your earthly masters with deep respect and fear. Serve them sincerely as you would serve Christ. Work hard, but not just to please your masters when they are watching. As slaves of Christ, do the will of God with all your heart. Work with enthusiasm, as though you were working for the Lord rather than for people. Remember that the Lord will reward each one of us for the good we do, whether we are slaves or free" (Ephesians 6:5–8, NLT).

INDIVIDUALITY

Most men think that in order to gain momentum in life they need to do something outrageous or grand. That's the deception modeled by pop culture to our young men.

The only way to get attention is to become a caricature or a ludicrous distortion of character traits. In their attempt to be noticed, young men begin to take on artificial mannerisms. They may overemphasize their flesh. They may pierce or tattoo their bodies in an attempt to make their mark on their surroundings. Their individuality is lost. They take the original intent of authenticity and sell out to a glossed, false image.

Man must realize that his contribution to the world will not come from copycat strategies but from digging deep into God's original intent for him. This revelation doesn't come from what is seen or heard, it comes from a secret place, from the inner streams of man's spirit (1 Corinthians 2:11).

What you do in secret is what moves you in public.

The Spirit led Jesus into isolation. For forty days and nights, He was isolated from all human contact, from food, and from water. It is interesting that after forty days, the voice that approached Him was Satan quoting scripture.

Although Jesus was the Word made flesh, His flesh was hungry and thirsty. You and I both know that the stomach has a powerful command over our actions. Hunger is a driving force in our lives. As Solomon said, *"Everything that man does is for his stomach"* *(Proverbs 16:26, author's paraphrase)*

Before Jesus went public, He first went into isolation.
Before the Apostle Paul went into public ministry, he spent three years in the isolation of Arabia (Galatians 1:11–18).

Before you can expect to reach your potential and make your mark, you will be forced into isolation. You cannot conquer the world unless you first conquer yourself.

Success is realized when preparation meets opportunity.

When the prophet came to David's home to anoint the next king of Israel, David wasn't even invited to the ceremony. He had too many responsibilities, tending his father's sheep.

One by one, the Spirit of God rejected each of David's seven brothers. The prophet became confused. Samuel knew the voice of God had specifically said, "Go to the home of Jesse and anoint the king of Israel," so he asked, "Do you not have another son?"

David was summoned out of the pasture of preparation in order to stand before the prophet. When the Spirit acknowledged David, oil was poured upon his head, and he was anointed the next king of Israel.

THE TENT OF TRAINING

When we are young and we experience a promise, we naïvely think that it should come to pass immediately; however, many times in the process, God moves us through training.

Many young men have high ambitions. Some want to embark on their conquests in their conceit and "make their mark." Others have clearly defined goals such as "to make my first million in my twenties, and first billion in my thirties."

Yeah, right.

David returned and served patiently in the pasture until he was called up to the tent of King Saul. Although Saul started out his reign with humility, his insecurities began to haunt his mind, and he became delusional, taking upon himself demonic suggestions.

There is hardly anyone more dangerous than a delusional leader. Saul became tormented, confused, and depressed. He found that music was a soothing reprieve from the voices within him, so he called for a musician. Once again, David's preparation met opportunity. His musical skills and prophetic psalms became just what the doctor ordered for Saul. But there was also a mutual benefit for David to serve in the tent. It became his tent of training.

While serving King Saul, David was able to observe the daily routine and decisions that leadership required. He was a witness to the stress of the throne. He saw how a king managed his men, his cabinet, and his family; although, in this case he primarily learned how not to lead.

"Unless you've been faithful to another man's possession, you are not qualified to manage your own" (Luke 16:12, author's paraphrase).

Even champions need a coach.

When you are a player, you need a coach. A coach helps draw out the skills that are within you. Even champions need a coach.

Tiger Woods was already on track to be a legend on the golf course. His skills had been carefully conditioned since childhood. He had already proven himself to be the number-one-ranked golfer when his coach changed his swing! Every commentator questioned the wisdom of Tiger's coach, and they questioned Tiger for putting his trust in another man to monkey with his proven skills.

Solomon said, *"When the axe is dull, more skill is required"* (Ecclesiastes 10:10, author's paraphrase).

Within a few months, the decision to change the fundamentals of Tiger Woods' swing proved to be a smart one. Tiger began to rely upon technique more than just his brute strength in hitting the ball. Without this fundamental change, his coach argued that Tiger's career would not last a lifetime but would fade out when injury and conditioning couldn't keep up with his age.

There are times on the field of contest that you must be willing to listen to a coach. **You must allow yourself to be trained.**

If you're going to ride a Harley, you should go with a seasoned rider to learn from his experience. Many guys have crushed themselves or even died because of their pride and unwillingness to learn the skill of safe riding.

If you want to do anything on the field of contest, it's better to get some training. It will make your experience better. Don't assume that you know what to do and how to do it. If you're taking up a sport, learn the rules of the game. Obviously, you will check out the proper attire and equipment, but more important than that, learn the etiquette of the game.

I made the mistake of playing golf for years before my wife surprised me with a series of lessons. That forced me to submit to a coach. I still review what I learned from Coach Ken every time I go to the driving range. My game improved considerably, and my enjoyment level on the golf course became even better.

(Incidentally, one of the plans that we have for Fivestarman is to not only host local, but also regional and national excursions, where men can express their adventurous spirits and enter the field of contest together. You can get more information on Fivestarman Excursions at the end of this book.)

DAVID'S FIELD OF CONTEST

The anointing oil had long since dried from David's head. You can imagine how patient and dedicated David had to be to hear the prophecy of Samuel only to return to the pasture and tend to his father's sheep. He showed complete humility to serve in the tent of the rejected king and then in being asked to deliver lunch to his elder brothers.

In obedience, David arrived at the Judean lowland where the army of Israel had gathered against their nemesis, Goliath, and the army of the Philistines.

The Philistines were not from a nation that bordered Israel, but a people of strife within the borders fighting over the same lands. The armies had aligned for battle. Boisterous and blasphemous ridicule came from the Philistines. They backed up their threats by sending out their champion, one of the last remaining descendants of the Nephilim, giants known as The Rejects. These brutes were known for their conquests. They were fearsome and dangerous. The Nephilim hated the Jewish people; it was the Jews who dislodged them from the land. They had tasted the grapes of the Promised Land but suffered the curse of displacement at the hands of the Israelites.

Goliath had been warring against God's people from his youth. His arrogant trash-talk was as boastful as his size. He was at least nine- and possibly eleven-feet tall, which translated into about 400 to 500 pounds of flesh. His armor alone weighed over 125 pounds.

This was the scene that David witnessed on the field of contest, the trembling army of Israel being led by their phobic King Saul. No one dared to take the giant up on his challenge. No one bought into the temptation to take the king up on his offer. The Israelite who would take out Goliath was to gain three very important rewards:

WEALTH—He would gain a transfer of wealth that would forever change his status in life. It would usher him and his family into a new way of living in a very difficult time.

TAX FREEDOM—The winner would be exempt from taxes for life. This special status alone would have been worth the risk.

A ROYAL WEDDING—King Saul offered his beautiful daughter Michal to be married to the victor. A princess who is pampered, privileged, and prosperous is certainly a prize, but more important than that was the status that came with marrying into the royal lineage.

When David heard the mockery and blasphemy of Goliath, righteous indignation arose within him. He became motivated to shut the man up. Then David asked a very important question that very few people are willing to ask.

What will be done for the man?

An adventurous spirit is vital to your success in life. Adventure is the ingredient that moves us into action. If you do not nurture this in your life, you will become increasingly sedate. Your life will lose its potency.

Some men have just enough success that they can't get over it. One of the hardest challenges that a man will ever face is a little success. Comfort sets in if you are not careful.

The greatest temptation in life is comfort.

I believe that one of the reasons God put the adventurous spirit in man was so that he would take the risks that life requires.

The willingness to risk it all for the prize is a motivating factor. Risk answers the question, "Why?" when a man is willing to climb mountains, ski down dangerous slopes, jump out of airplanes, hunt beasts, break speed records, and any number of seemingly foolish adventures. It is in our DNA. It is who we are, how we are made, and what motivates us to get up and face the world.

David's reward was more in line with the prophecy that hovered over his destiny. This crisis was an opportunity for the anointing on David's life to be publicly revealed. By taking out the giant, David would marry into the royal lineage that would be required to become King of Israel.

"NEVER LET A CRISIS GO TO WASTE."
—RAHM IMMANUEL

The size of your enemy determines the size of your reward.

THREE REWARDS FOR FACING GIANT CHALLENGES:

1. GREAT WEALTH
- You must be a problem solver.
- Your gains in life are in direct proportion to the problems that you solve.
- Look for problems that others are avoiding.
- Necessity is the mother of invention.
- Look for ways to be paid residually from the problems that you solve.
- You will never become rich while remaining comfortable.
- To get something that you've never had you must do something that you've never done.

2. SPECIAL STATUS
- Influence is a key to enlarging your rewards in life.
- Influence is a currency that is better than money.

- Influence is not fame. Fame is fleeting. Influence is legendary.
- Influence opens doors that are shut to others.

3. ROYAL LINEAGE
- A decision today can affect your descendants forever.
- Stepping up to the challenge can redirect your future.
- The prophecies and promises of your childhood will be revealed on the field of contest.

David stepped onto the field of contest that day to face his giant. It was on that day that the anointing on his life was revealed. It was on that day when a boy became a man, even "THE MAN." Goliath was a scourge on society that needed to be removed. Taking him out catapulted David into his destiny.

When you face a crisis, you will move into new battles. Once you enter the field of contest and face the challenge, you will become addicted to the adrenaline of risk.

When David cut off the head of Goliath *(saving it for his wall, I suppose)*, he stood and lifted it as a sign to the Philistines. It was the symbol that their greatest opponent had entered the field of contest and won.

> ## "LIFE IS EITHER A DARING ADVENTURE OR IT IS NOTHING."
> —HELEN KELLER

The adventurous spirit resides deep within authentic man and it requires expression. Many times you find that the man who regularly lives with the expression of adventure also experiences great gain in the financial world.

The field of contest is often transferable to the marketplace. A man who is motivated to take risks on the field often is often also motivated to take the necessary risks that accumulate great wealth.

THE GREATEST DAY

It would be difficult to find a more adventurous spirit than that found in the 26th President of the United States, Theodore "Teddy" Roosevelt. Although he was a sickly child, he began to overcome his ailments through exercise, taking up boxing. He was not much of an athlete, but he became a true outdoorsman and naturalist. His life story could not be told without including the field of contest as his playground. After being advised by his physician to choose a calming job due to his weak heart, Teddy chose to adopt a very strenuous lifestyle instead, becoming an adventurer.

Roosevelt owned two ranches, one in the Badlands of the Dakota Territory, the other just north of the settlement in Medora, North Dakota. When he was robbed, he chased down and captured the thieves who stole his boat. Rather than hanging them, he guarded them for over forty hours, safely returning them to the law to face trial.

While on his honeymoon in London, Roosevelt led a party to the summit of Mont Blanc, which earned him the accolades of the British Royal Society.

Known for his "Speak softly and carry a big stick" philosophy of leadership, he became a remarkable public servant.

In all of his accomplishments, exploits, and adventures, President Roosevelt said that the "great day of my life" was July 1, 1898, when he led the "Rough Riders" in the battle up Kettle Hill and San Juan Hill during the Spanish-American War, for which he would later receive the Medal of Honor posthumously.

It is the field of contest where men experience something that is intangible. Roosevelt's memories were filled with achievement, but he marked the "great day" of his life as a day of war.

THE CAVE OF CONFLICT

The next stage of David's adventure moved him into the cave of conflict.

After David defeated Goliath, Israel was motivated to defeat the Philistine army. When David returned victoriously, the girls came out joyously, singing spontaneous ditties about the young warrior hero. *"Saul has slain his thousands, and David his tens of thousands"* *(1 Samuel 18:7).*

You can imagine the deep root of bitterness that gripped King Saul. He then made the tragic mistake that leaders often do. He began to think that his enemies were within his own ranks rather than across the field of contest. Anytime this position is taken, destruction is imminent.

Saul began to despise the favor of God that was so evident upon young David. "Who is this guy, and where did he come from?" Saul asked.

This is always the wrong question that delusional leaders ask. It's not important to know where a person came *from*, but where he is *going* is what really matters.

David escaped the tentacles of Saul's revenge and found the cave of Adullam.

> *"David left Gath and escaped to the cave of Adullam. When his brothers and his father's household heard about it, they went down to him there. All those who were in distress or in debt or discontented gathered around him, and he became their leader. About four hundred men were with him.*
>
> *"From there David went to Mizpah in Moab and said to the king of Moab, 'Would you let my father and mother come and stay with you until I learn what God will do for me?' So he left them with the king of Moab, and they stayed with him as long as David was in the stronghold"* (1 Samuel 22:1–4).

Often, when you are in the cave of conflict, other conflicted people will be attracted to you. Those who were in distress, in debt, and discontented gathered around David.

Any gathering of men requires a leader.

Adullam means *justice of the people.* People who had faced the injustices of life sought equity, and as social outcasts, they needed a leader. They were in debt, discontent, and distressed, yet David turned them into the famed, "Mighty Men of David."

Their exploits are remarkable. One fought a lion in a pit on a snowy day. Another slew three hundred men in one standing.

> *"Some Gadites defected to David at his stronghold in the desert. They were brave warriors, ready for battle and able to handle the shield and spear. Their faces were the faces of lions, and they were as swift as gazelles in the mountains"* (1 Chronicles 12:8).

These men were not great men until David drew upon the purposes within them. It is the deep streams of purpose that make a man great.

You must have understanding of the deep streams of purpose within you. Conflict in your life can reveal the anointing upon you.

7 SECRETS TO BECOMING A MIGHTY MAN IN THE CAVE OF CONFLICT:

1. **AS LONG AS YOU LIVE, YOU WILL FACE AN ADVERSARY.**
   Most Western Christians think that opposition is a sign of a loss of favor, while globally, Christians interpret opposition as *favor*! Count it pure joy my brothers!

2. **YOU MUST RECOGNIZE THAT SATAN, THE NEMESIS OF MAN, IS YOUR ONLY TRUE ENEMY.**
   He uses weak and immature people to resist you, but he is your real enemy. The only way a spiritual force can operate in the earthly realm is when a person with a body yields to his will. Don't underestimate the power of simple-minded men.

3. YOUR SUFFICIENCY IS NOT WITHIN YOURSELF.

David encouraged himself in the Lord.

4. YOU MUST DECIDE TO FIGHT.

Most people cower. Most people are intimidated by the attack of the enemy.

5. YOU MUST PROVE YOUR ARMOR (EPHESIANS 6:13).

6. YOU MUST BE TEACHABLE AND CAPABLE OF LETTING GO OF A VICTIM'S MENTALITY.

You will either gain wisdom through pain or through mentorship. Choose mentorship.

7. MOTIVATE YOURSELF BY REMEMBERING THE REWARDS THAT AWAIT YOU (REVELATION 3:21).

THE BALCONY OF BOREDOM

I believe that one of the greatest challenges of modern man is boredom. Men who forfeit their place on the field of contest become bored with their lives.

Boredom is insidious. It gradually grips you in a stranglehold. It is an emotion that slowly suffocates you into a lazy, sluggish, lethargic coma.

As we discovered, King David was a man of the field. Later in life, after he had proven himself on that field and in subsequent wars, a haunting portion of Scripture stands out.

> *"In the spring, at the time when kings go off to war, David sent Joab out with the king's men and the whole Israelite*

army. They destroyed the Ammonites and besieged Rabbah. But David remained in Jerusalem.

"One evening David got up from his bed and walked around on the roof of the palace. From the roof he saw a woman bathing. The woman was very beautiful, and David sent someone to find out about her...." (2 Samuel 11:1–3).

David was pulled off the field of contest because his advisers feared the risks involved in the possible loss of their leader.

How does the lion's heart of a warrior spend his nights when others are on the field of contest?

In boredom, primarily.

David gave himself over to apathy. He began to wander on the balcony of boredom. From his perch, he lustfully looked upon a beautiful woman. The *victor* became the *voyeur*.

Most men commit adultery, not for the relationship, but for the risk. Their appetite is for risk, yet they forfeit their adventures for adolescent dreams.

David's boredom led to a series of tragic events. He summoned the beautiful woman into his bed, impregnated her, and then, to cover up his indiscretion, he actually exposed her husband, (a righteous man on the field of contest) to be killed by the sword of the Ammonites.

The seer Nathan exposed David's sins and spoke the dirge of prophecy, *"You are the man!"*

With this shocking exposé, Nathan went on to say, *"Out of your own household I am going to bring calamity upon you. Before your very eyes I will take your wives and give them to one who is close to you, and he will lie with your wives in broad daylight. You did it in secret, I will do this thing in broad daylight"* (2 Samuel 12:11–12).

What you do in secret is what moves you in public.

Take note: *The gate that you open is the one the enemy walks through.* If you open yourself up to pornography, it will become the arena where your family is exposed. This is not something to play with. You're not getting away with it, and it will cost you! Pornography is not a victimless crime. It is the sin of adultery.

This all started with boredom.

I am amazed at the apathy that has crept into manhood. We have plenty of opportunities to be on the field of contest, yet we have surrendered ourselves to become fat, lazy, unconditioned, and bored.

We need a different spirit for our manhood. We need to resurrect the spirit of adventure. Men will never receive the rewards of life without the willingness to take on the risks to get them.

The people of Israel were on the border of the land that was promised to them. They sent spies into the land to explore it. All twelve men returned with the report that the land was indeed exactly what God had promised—a land rich with produce and conditioned to provide for living large.

However, ten of the spies began to speak their fears. The critics paralyzed their manhood. Cowards in the crowd regurgitated their fears saying, *"We seemed like grasshoppers in their eyes."*

How could they know what they looked like in the eyes of the giants? Did they ask them?

Cowards always argue from this point of view. They say, *"People* are saying." Or they comment, *"Our critics* say. . ."

Who cares?! What does it matter what your enemy thinks of you? Only cowards think like that.

Caleb was one of two men who gave a good report of the land that he was sent to investigate. He also spoke words of encouragement saying, "We can do this!"

It's time to *stand up* and *speak up* to be a man. It's time that we reclaim the adventurous spirit.

The adrenaline of adventure will move you into authentic manhood, revealing greatness that is running in the streams of your purpose.

Get up! Get out there and do something that moves you! Do something risky.

PASSION TWO

ENTREPRENEURIAL DRIVE

PROLOGUE

The feeding frenzy seemed more like something that you would see on the African plains—hyenas laughing, devouring, and fighting over the latest scavenger hunt. But this feeding frenzy was the real estate market in the United States. It seemed almost magical, the ability to purchase properties that a few years earlier were completely out of reach for most upper-middle-class families. Young professionals thought of themselves as Trump tycoons buying cottages and condos, throwing in a little bit of paint, planting flowers, and then selling these parcels for extraordinary profits. These schemers devoured the weak and laughed all the way to the bank to prepare for the next hunt. And the banks loved it. They shuffled the paper, overlooked the details, and slid the half-baked mortgages into portfolios of junk loans to be pawned off to the federally backed Fannies and Freddies.

Eric and his wife, Katrina, spent their afternoons and Saturdays going to open houses, scouring the Internet, and listening to their friends talk about the latest great deal. Every social gathering became awkward for Eric. He looked at a hundred homes, it seemed, but he couldn't ever pull the trigger to make a purchase. He had already been approved at the bank for more than five times his annual salary. The numbers didn't add up in his mind. "How can this possibly be real?" he would reason out loud. His best friend, Peter, kept adding to his portfolio of properties, which added to the pressure on Eric to dive into the frenzy. Peter was living large, living the dream, buying new cars, and taking exotic vacations, all on the margin of mortgages and liberally appraised homes.

Although Katrina would have loved to be in a bigger home, or even to have the condo at the beach, she trusted Eric. He had always had a strong work ethic. The couple fared rather well, had some money in the bank, and enjoyed a good life. The challenge was thinking that they were the only ones who were not in the mix of this new Western expansion. Their doubts persisted until the fall of 2008, when the bubble burst and the fall out of crashing homes tumbled down in the inevitable "correction." Their friends' fantasies came crashing down with it. Peter lost everything; his "houses of cards" came down, as did his lifestyle.

Eric felt relieved and soberly grateful that he hadn't taken the plunge into what seemed to be a gold mine of quick profits. Katrina was grateful that she had trusted her husband and that his wisdom had protected their family.

ENTREPRENEURIAL DRIVE   **61**

ENTREPRENEURIAL DRIVE

One of the most intriguing men that I've ever met is David Green, founder and CEO of Hobby Lobby. His merchant skills are evident if you've ever walked through one of the nearly 500 stores that Hobby Lobby operates in thirty-nine states. He is a true entrepreneur, a man who took a $600 investment and turned it into more than a $1.5 billion dollar a year success. I highly recommend that you read his book, **More Than a Hobby** (*Nelson Business, Thomas Nelson Publishing, Inc., Nashville, TN,* © *2005*). It is one of the most insightful books written by a CEO that I've ever read.

David Green didn't begin his career after receiving a business degree from an ivy-league business school; quite the opposite, he earned his credentials through a work-study program of his local middle school, at McClellan's Store in Altus, Oklahoma.

The principles that have guided David Green's success are so simple, yet they confound the wise. They are:

1. Run your business in harmony with God's laws.
2. Focus on people, not money.
3. Be a merchant, which means buying and selling merchandise.
4. Install systems that protect the integrity of the first three.

David has ingeniously narrowed the principles of success down to the simplest form of understanding.

The entrepreneurial drive that is within you is a stream of purpose that must be drawn upon. It is a deep sense of financial purpose.

In order to gain understanding of the entrepreneurial drive, we must revisit some of the original intent of how God made man.

MAN IS THE ECONOMY

You can't read the Bible without this theme echoing through the pages: "Scatter upon the Earth. Populate it. Dominate it. Subdue it. Go into all the world!" This is God's consistent message to mankind; yet, the recurring theme of man is the opposite. Man always wants to settle, to be comfortable, to not want too much.

In the book of Genesis, when mankind advanced eastward and found the plain of Shinar and settled there, they said, *"Come, let's make bricks and bake them thoroughly" (Genesis 11:3).*

Man began to use ingenuity to develop resources. Instead of gathering stones, men invented bricks, and they used tar for mortar. Men drew from within themselves to invent technologies to replace the limitations of the natural resources available.

Then they said, *"Come, let us build ourselves a city, with a tower that reaches to the heavens, so that we may make a name for ourselves and not be scattered over the face of the whole earth." (Genesis 11:4).*

Their entrepreneurial drive was tapped to engineer a city and architecturally design a tower.

God's response to the Tower of Babel often surprises people. He said, *"If as one people speaking the same language they have begun to do this, then nothing they plan to do will be impossible for them"* *(Genesis 11:6).*

That's an amazing compliment. God witnessed the incredible ability within man, and He bragged about it!

Theirs was a perfectly designed mission statement. It was specific, concise, clear, articulate, and motivating.

Many people have argued that man was attempting to build himself a stairway to Heaven by designing the tower. I don't see that. What leaps out at me is the thought in verse 4, *"So that we are not scattered over the face of the whole earth."*

When God confused men's ability to understand one another, the result was that they were scattered. Solomon said, "Men make plans but God's purpose prevails." God used this confusion to cause man to return to His original intent.

It has always been God's desire for man to dominate the whole Earth.

As I discussed earlier, the propaganda of our time is a constant barrage of anti-human expansion upon the Earth. Population control—whether by abortion, euthanasia, or genocide—is the secret strategy of many elite theorists that has seized control of organizations around the world. It is all based upon the lie of popular economics, saying: The world contains a limited supply of physical resources (land, oil, gas, minerals, etc.), and wealth is determined by the control and management of those resources.

This premise as a foundational thought creates a chain reaction of erroneous pursuits. It is an amazing flaw in the thinking of secular man. Just as in the story of the Tower of Babel, today people are working their plans against God's original intent, and they will fail. There is no scheme or strategy that can succeed against the Lord.

Man has a nemesis, a satanic spirit that works against the original intent for man. This principality is constantly scheming to resist the advancement of man. He works in our culture, our government, our media, and by every available means he can to resist you.

In fact, he has persuaded man to adopt the religious idea to not want "too much" material wealth in this life. The lie of scarcity leads to the false theology that God does not want man to prosper. Don't stumble over the word *prosper*. It's a biblical word that is useful, if you understand it. It means that *your journey will go well with you; that you will dwell safely and, with provision, fulfill your purpose.*

Before you overreact and call me a heretic, take a deep breath and reason with me for a moment.

As a father, do you personally desire that your children and grandchildren live healthy and wealthy lives? Do you want your child to have a quality education that enables him or her to pursue a life even better than you have enjoyed? Do you want your kids to have the freedoms that health provides? Do you want your child to have a safe and comfortable home to dwell in? A place where memories of family resonate with holidays that were filled with laughter and good food?

Of course you want that kind of life for your children. I would argue that there is something wrong with you if you don't want that for your children. But that is exactly what the slander against God is proclaiming, that we know how to give good gifts to our children, but God wants us to be poor! That's a hypocritical and silly argument. It's a blight against the character of the omnipotent God. God is wise enough to put on deposit enough material wealth for all of mankind throughout all the ages to live and to thrive. The only way you can argue against financial prosperity is if you have a scarcity mentality. To make such a claim means that you do not believe that God is a rewarder of those who seek Him (Hebrews 11:6).

Unless you get over the untruth of the poverty mentality, you will never understand the deep stream of the entrepreneurial drive that is within you.

I will not waste my time to defend the excessive greed of a few preachers who have distorted the biblical word *prosperity*. If a man begins to name his "stuff," a churning takes place in my stomach. He obviously believes that gain equals godliness. Please don't get me wrong on this. I have personally invested all of my income on several occasions to advance the purpose for which God has called me to accomplish. I can agree with Paul, *"I have had much and I have had little, and I have learned the secret of being content in all situations"* (Philippians 4:12, author's paraphrase). But, I refuse to slander God's character by saying that He is not a holy, good, and loving Father who wants His children to prosper.

Most men struggle with the scarcity mentality within the church, so they choose simply not to attend. Many are content to make the money, so that their wives and children can "have religion." It is hard to reason with the preacher who argues from his own perspective of "sacrificial poverty." His manhood resonates within him, "I must provide for my family," but in his mind to become a Christian means to take on a vow of poverty. He can't reconcile both lines of thinking, and he lives in confusion.

Centuries ago, the religious system decided that in order for the church to advance, its ministers should take vows of poverty. Priests were to deny themselves so that the bureaucrats of centralized religion could better control the collection plate. They added that priests should also refrain from marriage in order to save the church even more expense. This is a sadistic theology that has no biblical basis. This twisting of God's Word for their own ambition led to a priesthood of perverts.

There are a few Scriptures that are used to justify the argument that we should not accumulate wealth. I get that. But we must look at those Scriptures in the light of the context in which they are taught.

OPPORTUNITY LOST

The rich young ruler who had lived a life of incredible devotion to the laws of God and had practiced discipline in finances was encouraged by Jesus, *"Go sell your possessions, give it to the poor, you will transfer your wealth into heaven. Then come, follow me"* (Mark 10:21, author's paraphrase).

Jesus' next statement is the one used by those who argue against having any wealth, *"How hard is it for the rich to enter the kingdom of God!"*

This is where most scarcity-minded theologians stop the story.

But the disciples asked a probing question, *"Who then can be saved?"*

The question is good because it begs for understanding. "Who determines what is rich?"

If poverty is holy, then why do we fight against it? Why don't we go to the poorest of the poor and learn from them?

I don't despise the poor, but I hate poverty. I hate what it does to humanity. I hate how insidious it is. I hate the advantage poverty has over people who are created to rise above it. Poverty is an evil that strangles people. It robs them of opportunity, education, clothing, shelter, nourishment, health, joyful living, independence, and family.

Jesus' response to that question helped the disciples, *"No one who has left home or brothers or sisters or mother or father or children or fields for me and the gospel will fail to receive a hundred times as much in this present age, . . . and in the age to come, eternal life"* (Mark 10:29).

Jesus instructs us to invest our talents and resources into eternal matters—which is people. This Earth will pass away, and only what has been invested in people will take on the substance of eternity. *(We'll cover this principle in more detail when we cover your legacy and the philanthropic cause.)*

What Jesus makes clear to the disciples is that the rich young ruler should have waited to hear the rest of the story. As a wise young man, he would have heard that if he would invest in giving to the poor, his wealth would immediately accumulate a hundred times more than what it was valued at, and he would have also become a disciple who followed Jesus.

This nameless young man could have been "named" in the Twelve. Jesus knew that the treasurer of His ministry would betray Him. He knew that Judas would need to be replaced. Who better to replace a thief than a proven young financial genius like the rich young ruler?

What a tragic loss!

This is where many men find themselves, walking away from the call to follow Jesus, because they misunderstand the call. Authentic manhood dictates that men must provide for their own families, yet the church (not the Bible) tells them that they must be poor to be holy. So a man's response to this philosophy may be, "Then I'll just provide for my family and go to hell, so that they're taken care of and can go to Heaven."

My grandfather was that kind of man. He couldn't reconcile in his mind how he could do both—provide for his family and also be a Christian who believed that he must be poor! It wasn't until he was eighty-nine years old, when I convinced him about the love of Christ that he accepted Jesus as Savior.

It's great that my grandfather got saved a few months before his death, but it's tragic that he lived his whole life without the benefits of the Good News.

God equips you and expects you to be productive.

In Matthew 25, Jesus told a story about a man who had prepared for an excursion. As all good entrepreneurs, he called in his management team and assigned each one of them a portfolio to manage and grow. He dispersed his wealth among them according to their proven abilities. After a season of time, he returned to get an accounting of his resources. The first manager doubled his wealth. The second doubled his wealth. The third employee *maintained* his wealth.

The entrepreneur's response was an enlightening glimpse into the character of God. The entrepreneur responded to the first two managers in the same manner, *"You have proven yourself, I will reward you openly and acknowledge your success, even sharing in the profits."* His response to the maintainer was very different. *"You're fired!"*

We are sometimes deceived into thinking that maintenance is honorable. It's not. It's worthy of termination. We are designed for increase. Anything short is simply below our status.

Unless you return to God's original intent for you, you will never have the confidence to draw upon the entrepreneurial drive.

The maintainer argued that his lack of productivity was because of the character of the master rather than the insecurity, fear, and laziness that was within himself. That's exactly the same argument of the one who has a scarcity mentality. He blames God!

It's within our DNA to expect results. It is ridiculous to argue against it. Maintenance brings death to resources. It is the nature of the Earth to increase.

SEED IS CURRENCY

When God created the Earth, he established a global currency. The currency is a principle, more than it is a single substance. Let me explain.

God created the earth to operate on the principle of Seedtime and Harvest (what I call, "STH"). He established STH as the economic system for as long as the Earth remains. Yet, few people realize that it is more of an economic system than it is produce.

Whatever you assign to the STH system returns with the same result—increase!

Dollar, Yen, Euro, Franc, Peso, gold, or silver—whatever cultures use as their currency—everything works on the principle of STH. In the same way that the men of Shinar in Genesis 11 made brick instead of stone, we've used dollars instead of gold. They all work on the principle of STH.

Rather than having your confidence in a particular currency of man, you should realize that seed is the currency that God established for the Earth. By trusting in the seed, you will diminish your trust in pieces of paper with dead presidents embossed on them and have confidence that "Whatever you sow, that shall you also reap."

"THE CORE ACTIVITY IS BUYING AND SELLING MERCHANDISE."
—DAVID GREEN

This will relieve you of a fundamental mistake that most entrepreneurs make. They get their eye off the ball and begin to focus on money, rather than people. Remember, man is the economy. Without another person to make the exchange, there is no purpose for money.

When companies begin to focus on money rather than people, they issue policies that are more convenient to the organization than the customer. They lose sight of the fact that without the customer, they have no reason for existence. You can have barrels of money, and yet, without the economic systems of STH, it's all useless.

THE PROMISE

The entrepreneurial drive is best displayed in the life of Abraham.

Abraham's father, Terah had the internal drive to move his family to a prosperous land filled with unlimited resources, namely the land of Canaan. As Terah traveled with his family, he paused for a brief stop in the city of Haran. The city was a memorial to Terah's son Haran, who had died much too early in life.

At Haran, settling stopped the progress of man. Haran became a shrine for Terah and he couldn't move forward into what God had planned for his life.

There are lessons to learn about tragedy:
1. Tragedy happens.
2. Don't spend your life as a memorial for the dead.
3. You must be willing to let the dead go and move forward toward your destiny.

Terah couldn't get over the death of his son, so he took up residence at Haran. When a man will not move forward in progress, God has no choice but to call upon someone else to pursue His plan.

God spoke to Abraham saying, *"Leave your country, your people and your father's household and go to the land I will show you"* (Genesis 12:1) Abraham had a choice. He could stay and dwell in his father's misery, or he could move out and trust the voice of God to lead him. Abraham did not know where his obedience would take him, but he trusted that the Lord had ordered his steps.

God's promise to Abraham can be summed up in this statement, *"Go to the land I will show you."*

Abraham became the first person to use land as a commodity to be exchanged. He discussed the price of the property, defined its boundaries by legal description, and made the transaction a public notice. This became the foundation for real estate transactions even until today.

God's promise to Abraham was that "all nations" would be blessed through Abraham. God transformed Abraham's thinking from a nomadic gatherer to a landowner/seed-sower. Nomads relied upon what the Earth produced on its own. They were scavengers at nature's mercy, but Abraham began to sow seeds for a determined future.

This is the key to the entrepreneurial drive. The entrepreneur believes in his abilities to determine his financial future through innovative and systematic efforts. The entrepreneur believes that he can improve his own position in life by his abilities and God's promise to be blessed.

Solomon said, *"He who works his land will have abundant food, but the one who chases fantasies will have his fill of poverty"* (*Proverbs 28:19*).

Notice that abundance comes from the STH process, while the "chaser" experiences lack and mere subsistence.

Sometimes men make the mistake of being "nomadic" in employment. They scavenge where there is work. That is certainly an option, but it becomes unreliable in the long term. They're constantly chasing the next dollar.

The best option is to follow Abraham's example and to own property rights, using those rights to practice STH.

Property ownership is the promise that God made to Abraham, "Go to the land that I will show you." Occupying and having rights to this particular piece of real estate (Israel) has been the cause of innumerable wars. Even today, the news is consumed by the argument over this same piece of land. Yet, I would argue that it is not only the geographical plot of land that is the point of contention, but also, it is the individual right to own property in the first place.

Once again, the nemesis of man is attempting to take this fundamental right out of man's control and put it into the control of a few elites of the governing class. The book of Revelation reveals that this will begin the hostile takeover of economic control exercised over the population of the end times. Eliminating the right to own property, whether real or intellectual, is the key to personal prosperity and is the promise God made to Abraham.

The economy is driven by the ability of an entrepreneur to possess real or intellectual property.

God is wise enough to deposit within man the ability to provide for and prosper him to accomplish His purpose upon the Earth. The individual right to own and manage personal property is the key to individual prosperity.

Matt White was the first billionaire baseball player; however, he didn't make his money through baseball. He made it by helping out a family member in need. Matt was a struggling pitcher with the Los Angeles Dodgers when he purchased fifty acres of land from his aunt who needed to sell her property to move into a nursing home.

After the purchase, White hired a surveyor to inspect his land only to find that the land was solid Goshen stone, estimated to be worth over $2.5 billion.

This is a good example of how a man can dig deep to discover hidden riches.

It would be unimaginable for the Creator to design man without endowing him with the ability to sustain his family and succeed in life.

You have the ability within you to provide for your family.

You may not know it; you may not yet have understanding, but this ability is awaiting your discovery. Within every man is a gift, and that gift is for the common good. Others will benefit from your gift, and they will make a currency exchange for it.

Solomon said, *"The gift makes room for you, it ushers you into greatness"* (Proverbs 18:16, author's paraphrase).

I live with the conviction that every person on Earth has within him or her a gift for the good of mankind, but it requires understanding from the Creator for it to be used properly.

Your ability to make a living will be in direct proportion to your proficiency to draw out the divine deposit within you.

You must realize that an omniscient God designed you after His own image with sustenance inside you. When God spoke to the land, He said, *"Produce vegetation, trees, and seed!"* When God spoke to the oceans, He said, *"Teem with creatures!"* When God spoke to Himself, He said, *"Let us make man in our own image."*

You must know your Source. When you know your Source, you will discover your potential.

As an entrepreneur, you have the ability to dig deep within your spirit to discover the Source—the God-given, inspired, crafted ability to, not only make a living, but to fulfill your life.

STIR IT UP!

You have a gift. That's an absolute, not for debate. You were created in the "shadowed" image of God. You were created with a unique gift to contribute to humanity, and that gift has the mutual benefit of returning a supply into your life. You must first recognize the gift.

Men often don't recognize their gift because it is disguised as something ordinary. What comes easy to some men often causes them to assume that everyone can do what they do, making their gifting unrecognizable. This is a fundamental mistake of man.

I have seen this in raising my three children. I noticed that their extraordinary gifts seemed to be so natural, so evident, that they didn't embrace them as unique abilities given to them by God.

Many times you must stir up the gift within you or others for it to be recognized as extraordinary.

When Moses received the revelation to build a very special tent, he lacked the necessary skill to do it himself, yet he found that God had especially equipped a man to do the work, namely Bezalel, which means *shadow of God*. The Bible says God filled Bezalel *"with the Spirit of God, with skill, ability, and knowledge in all kinds of crafts—to make artistic designs for work in gold, silver, and bronze, to cut and set stones, to work in wood and to engage in all kinds of artistic craftsmanship" (Exodus 35:31–33).*

Even though Moses received the blueprints of the tabernacle, it was Bezalel who received the unique ability to fulfill the plan.

Some people believe that to be an entrepreneur you must be completely independent, when in fact, the complete opposite is true.

The entrepreneurial drive within you is especially designed to connect you with others. To be entrepreneurial in spirit means that you are a master networker, connecting yourself with other very talented and gifted individuals to accomplish shared benefits. You can't go it alone. You may receive an incredible idea, yet without the right network of skilled people, you will never be able to bring it into being.

Release your gift!

Don't be the Lone Ranger; don't think that just because God gave you an idea you must do all of the work. That's not how God works. He works through the networking of people to bring things to pass. No man is an island. You can't do it all.

When God told me, "Build a movement to resurrect authentic manhood," I knew that I would need to recruit gifted men to lay the foundation for Fivestarman. Even though I may have received the original instruction, I had to pass it on to others. It is our goal to give away this message until it becomes a global movement of men resurrecting authentic manhood.

The same will be true for you. When you receive an idea, ask God to bring you connected partners to labor with you. Jesus said, *"Look at the fields; they are ready to harvest. Ask for workers." (See John 4:35 and Luke 10:2.)*

I can't tell you how frustrating it is to see skilled men lay down their abilities and talents. I have seen good men retire when they should have just re-ignited!

I don't expect to retire. There's no future in it.

You should try to avoid it, too. When men retire from work, they sit down near a stream and fade away. Forget it! You have too much purpose to retire!

When my father "retired" to a mountain in Arkansas, he took down some old notes that he had written years earlier. On these notes were the seeds of stories, historical Western novels. Although it stretched him, he went out and purchased a computer. He learned how to turn it on and began to type out his first novel. He adopted the pen name of "Dusty Rhodes." He joined a writer's club and shared his drafts to be scrutinized by other members. As difficult as that was, he listened and sharpened his skills. He published his first book as an e-book, an electronic version only. When he won a prestigious electronic-publishing award, a publishing company printed his book.

Every weekend, my father would attend Arts and Crafts shows all over the heartland of Oklahoma, Arkansas, Texas, New Mexico, and Colorado. Soon, people began to line up to purchase his book.

Now, near his eighties, and fourteen novels later, he continues to tell his stories, on average, writing a book a year.

Not only do I get to enjoy my father's books, I get to know him more by reading his stories. I know how he thinks and the values that he believes in and the God whom he serves. Although he didn't raise me, we now enjoy a good relationship that I honor.

DON'T EXCUSE YOURSELF

The last thing that you should consider is exiting the marketplace. Don't give yourself the excuse to run out the door. If you've failed, congratulations! I have never met nor read about any wealthy person who didn't experience tragic loss before achieving their greatness. I love reading the biographies of men who have failed. We love to hear these stories because they dig deep into the adventurous spirit of a man—the risk excites us.

There is no reward without risk.

Some men excuse themselves because of where they are from. What does that matter?

Some men excuse themselves because of their physical appearance. Are you kidding? Have you seen pictures of the past presidents? They're a rough bunch to look at.

Some men excuse themselves because of a lack of education. There's a huge difference between the uneducated and the ignorant. If you are ignorant, yes, you have a distinct disadvantage that you must overcome, either by finding a mentor and/or by making and learning from your mistakes.

If you are uneducated, that's easy to fix. Just remember that education will not fix everything. It exposes more opportunities, but it doesn't always translate into wealth. As Dave Ramsey, a multimillion-dollar industry within himself, said, "I have PHD working for me!" Just because you have initials behind your name, that doesn't guarantee success. In fact, W. Randall Jones, author of *The Richest Man in Town: The Twelve Commandments of Wealth* *(Business Plus, Hachette Book Group, Inc., New York, NY, © 2009)*, said that only 10 percent of the one hundred people he interviewed for his book had an Ivy League education.

Men often excuse themselves from reading. Leaders are readers. The average millionaire reads more than three books a month. The average American *starts to read* one book a year, and *doesn't finish it!* You have access to more knowledge than anyone could have imagined a few years ago. Don't waste the opportunity. Read. Read. Read.

The Renaissance man Leonardo da Vinci fascinates me because he represented a true entrepreneur. Although he was illegitimately born the son of a notary and a peasant woman, he overcame a lack of privilege and education to become distinguished as a truly brilliant man. He was an artist, natural philosopher, engineer, and even a topographic anatomist—and one thing is for sure—Leo was an entrepreneur, drawing upon the gift of God within him to explore and develop himself financially.

Leonardo da Vinci recorded over 13,000 pages of journal entries, which included designs for a helicopter, weaponry and defense mechanisms, shoes for walking on water, a sprinkler system for a restaurant, hydraulic pumps, and hundreds of other practical inventions. He was a master at turning an idea into a commission payment.

In 1550, renowned artist and architect Giorgio Vasari wrote this of Leonardo da Vinci, in his book, *Lives Of The Most Excellent Painters, Sculptors, And Architects*:

> "In the normal course of events many men and women are born with remarkable talents; but occasionally, in a way that transcends nature, a single person is marvelously endowed by Heaven with beauty, grace and talent in such abundance that he leaves other men far behind, all his actions seem inspired, and indeed everything he does clearly comes from God rather than from human skill. Everyone acknowledged that this was true of Leonardo da Vinci, an artist of outstanding physical beauty, who displayed infinite grace in everything that he did and who cultivated his genius so brilliantly that all problems he studied he solved with ease."

Men often come up to me and say, "Neil, I've got this idea. I know it's worth a lot of money. I just don't know what to do with it. I am afraid to share it with anyone lest they steal it from me."

An idea is worth a dollar; a strategy is worth a million dollars.

If you get an idea, you must process it. You must let it simmer within you. Here are some steps you can take to process any idea:

1. BE CURIOUS.
Observe, study, and learn.

2. FIND A PROBLEM.

Your income is the result of solving problems.

3. WRITE IT DOWN.

Process it through the filter of blueprints or business plans. Journal your thoughts.

4. TEST IT.

Go through the process of trial and error.

5. PROTECT IT.

If you can, patent it or license it.

6. NETWORK IT.

If it is a good idea and solves a problem that everyone has, it has the ability to turn a profit.

As an authentic man, you have the entrepreneurial drive within you so that you can amply provide for your family and fulfill your purpose.

PASSION THREE

GALLANT IN RELATIONSHIPS

PROLOGUE

It could have been a sequence of the old, classic television series, *The Waltons*, when the family went through their evening ritual of saying good night; however, this family was very different.

Shawn, a young boy, raised his voice to say, "Good night, Dad. I love you."

"I love you too, Son. Good night."

The boy's sister, Dawn, offered her nightly salutation, "Good night, Dad. I love you."

The father remained silent. He could not make himself say it. His only reply was, "Night."

With tears in her eyes, the mother looked at him with disgust, "You can't even tell her that you love her?"

Dawn felt a loneliness that was frightening. To get through this night, just like every other night, a bitter root was buried deep within her, causing her to hate her father, and men altogether.

The subsequent divorce of her parents didn't help. The nighttime was still absent her father's voice. He wasn't there at all. When he came to visit his children, Shawn was the only one he picked up. Dawn stayed, looking out the bedroom window as they drove away. She buried her pain so deep that no man would be able to soothe it. Why did her father despise her? What was the hatred that he had toward her? Why was she the one feeling guilty, transferring his hatred toward herself?

As Dawn grew up, she dated, but no man could ever be trusted. Her relationships didn't have a chance to last. She went through marriages as fast as most people date. She didn't know what she was looking for. No man could fulfill her need. She was attracted to the same type of man every time—the bully, hard living, mysterious—the man who reminded her of her absentee father.

Like the woman at the well, whom Jesus spoke to concerning her failure in relationships, Dawn also drew from the depths, but her well was filled with bitter water.

And like that Samaritan woman, Dawn needed a Word to be spoken to penetrate the hard shell of resentfulness covering her broken heart.

When Dawn met David, he surprised her. He seemed to have a quiet confidence within himself, a calm demeanor, a resolve so attractive she couldn't resist wanting to know him. He was a good-looking man. His character and personality made him very handsome. David spoke to Dawn as if he already knew her. He seemed to be able to read her like a book. His words were not shallow or trivial but penetrating surgical instruments that were able to cut deep, so deep in fact, that she became frightened by his awareness of her.

'How can he know me?' she thought to herself.

During conversations, his eyes focused upon her. He would not even glance around the room. His attention was undivided. He listened. At times, it was awkward.

After each date, Dawn would determine to protect herself, worried that she was letting him get too deep. She had often used sex to manipulate men in order to control her relationships. She tried to seduce David, but he wouldn't take the bait.

"Dawn, I like you. I value who you are too much to misuse your trust in me. Let's get to know one another. Let's build a relationship on a stronger foundation than the physical."

She didn't realize the change in her appearance until one day when she looked into the mirror and realized that her skin seemed to be more flush, more alive. Her eyes were clearer; her skin was fresh and clean. Her hair and nails seemed to glow. She had dropped in weight to a trim and healthy number that she hadn't seen on the scale in years. She hadn't even been dieting. *What's happening to me?* she wondered. When her friends quizzed her about her new radiance, she just smiled and shrugged her shoulders.

The bitterness she had harbored like a treasured possession suddenly argued with her. *Don't think this guy loves you! He's only playing you to hurt you.* She tried to debate the inner voice but seemed overwhelmed by its power. Her anger was so strong against men that she snapped at David, "Who do you think you are? Who are you to come into my life only to hurt me? I won't allow you to control me!"

David's calm and soft answer was like a soothing massage, "Dawn, let go of the hurt your father caused you. I will never leave you. I will never hurt you. I will tuck you into bed each night and whisper in your ear, *'I love you.'*"

The gentle words he sowed into her heart caressed her pain and began to wipe away years of emotional scars.

GALLANT IN RELATIONSHIPS

I know that "gallant" is a word we don't use very often in our modern vernacular, but it's a word the authentic man will resurrect. To truly be gallant is a deep purpose of man. It draws upon one of the most amazing qualities that a man possesses, yet is rarely conditioned in modern culture.

To be *gallant* means *to show special attention and respect toward a woman in an honorable way.* It means that a man will treat an older woman as he would treat his own mother, a younger woman as his own daughter, and a woman who is his peer as his own sister. *Gallant* also means *to be heroic in the defense of the weak, such as a child or the elderly.* It is true chivalry.

This inner quality dictates a man's appearance. The gallant man is groomed, fashionable, and appropriately prepared for every occasion.

Gallantry is a stream that runs deep within authentic man. This quality is revealed in every action movie designed to appeal to men. The gallant hero fights against immeasurable odds with a damsel by his side the whole way. In the midst of flames and destruction, he finally kisses the girl. The special effects get larger and larger and the plot is always rooted in the same key component—there is always a woman to rescue.

Gallantry is the key ingredient in the movie *Braveheart* (which, by the way, is the ultimate "man movie"). Staged on the field of contest, William Wallace fights for the right to own personal property, revenging the love of his life, driven by principles of character and integrity, and leaving the legacy of his heir upon the throne of the British kingdom in the place of the effeminate royal despot.

As men, we must resurrect the authenticity of being gallant. **Our society is suffering from a lack of honorable conduct.** There was a time when men stood on the river banks to duel for the sake of honor—today, they drive by homes in the dark with machine guns blazing.

When I grew up in Oklahoma, we were taught that fighting was appropriate only for the sake of defending your honor. The only fights I was ever involved in were over my honor or for protecting a girl.

We've conditioned our boys not to stand up against the bully—we would rather "counsel" them. But there are irrational minds that appeasement can't convince. There are times when capitulation doesn't help. We must be willing to defend what is right.

To be gallant means that we respect and defend our dignity, the dignity of being a man, and the honor of a woman.

LIFE IS IN THE SEED

The Supreme Court made an irrational decision based upon a fraudulent case in Roe v. Wade, the decision that a woman has the "right to choose" whether or not she will carry a child within her protected womb until the day of delivery. She alone has the choice. The man doesn't have any say in the matter. Four decades later, more than 55 million children have been slaughtered within the sacred vault.

My argument against abortion predates the decision of "choice." As gallant men, we must raise our sons to value the life-giving seed within them so much that they are unwilling to deposit it into an unworthy woman.

We must stop saying that it is the woman's choice—**no, it is the young man's choice, and he will be held responsible for it.** He is responsible for the spillage of his seed.

Think about how important it is to be endowed with Life-Seed and compare that with the flippant attitude that men have toward it. Every men's magazine talks about sex as if it was simply an animalistic event, but the act is much more important than ejaculation. It is the deposit of life!

Solomon speaks of the seed of man as streams running in the public streets, *"Should your springs overflow in the streets, your streams of water in the public squares? Let them be yours alone, never to be shared with strangers"* (Proverbs 5:16–17).

The authentic man understands the dignity of being prudent with his seed.

The Bible speaks to this very fact when addressing the practice of *yibum* in the Hebrew culture—the principle of *establishing the family name.*

Judah had three sons with a Canaanite woman named Shua. Their first son, Er married Tamar, but he died of his wickedness. His brother Onan was instructed to step in to fulfill the Jewish law of Yibum, which was the law established to keep the lineage of Jewish men perpetuating.

> *"Onan knew that the offspring would not be his; so whenever he slept with his brother's wife, he spilled his semen on the*

ground to keep from producing offspring for his brother"
(Genesis 38:9).

This act of spillage was so wicked that Onan died. Obviously, men don't die every time they spill their seed on the ground, but it reiterates how importantly life-giving seed should be regarded. We must resurrect authentic manhood in regards to honoring man's ability to sow life into a woman.

You will not fulfill your purpose chasing after the latest conquest. You will die a miserable, spent, dried-up man. Any day of the week, a man can reduce himself to dishonor, but it takes an authentic man to protect his dignity.

PROXIMITY

Solomon warns the gallant man to keep his distance from the unworthy woman. He describes observing a young man, a simple and naïve guy, walking toward a woman's house at twilight. She came out of her house dressed to kill. She was loud and defiant. An accurate description of this woman in the Hebrew is that she was like an "untrained cow." Her brazen look captivated his imagination. She took him into her bed, which was freshly dressed with fragrances and oils. *"Let's drink in love with no regrets."*

Every men's magazine is filled with this type of woman—the brazen look, the busty, seductive eyes of a whore—leading men to the chambers of death (Proverbs 7).

Have some dignity. Control yourself as a man. Don't lower yourself into the ranks of the victims. Stand strong with your shoulders back and your honor held high.

Most of the battle is won simply by keeping a proper distance. Proximity is key to staying pure. Solomon warns of the woman's seductive words. Don't allow a woman to come near enough to touch you or to whisper in your ear.

A MAN OF DISPLEASURE

> *"The mouth of an immoral woman is a deep pit; those living under the LORD's displeasure will fall into it"*
> *(Proverbs 22:14, NLT).*

Most men have the assumption that sexual sin brings the judgment of God. While that is true, it is also clear that sexual sin **IS** the judgment of God. God allows a man who has not lived honorably to become trapped in sexual sin for the degrading of his body.

If a man is invested in sexual sin, he is revealing a fallen relationship with God. It isn't the cause of the displeasure; it is a result of displeasure.

Paul describes the process: *"God gave them over in the sinful desires of their hearts to sexual impurity for the degrading of their bodies with one another"* (Romans 1:24).

> *"The body is not meant for sexual immorality"*
> *(1 Corinthians 6:13).*

Sexual promiscuity is now the norm of our society. After the "sexual revolution," the prudent behavior of purity has become laughable in some circles, yet I believe that within the authentic man is a desire to remain a pure man. I believe that there are still men who want to live honorably and respect themselves at the highest degree.

Your body is not made for sexual immorality. Remember: **Where the purpose is unknown abuse is inevitable.** If you misuse your body for immorality, a destructive process begins to take place. Your body literally begins to experience a chemical breakdown when you submit it to sex outside the bounds of marriage.

The man who submits his body to immorality is literally sinning against his own body (1 Corinthians 6:18). The sight of a woman stimulates a man. If he is overexposed to that stimulation, the result is a dysfunction. Erectile dysfunction is a cultural phenomenon. I believe that the over exposure of women is the culprit that has caused this epidemic.

Some men think that they will discover love when they have sex. I know men who have reasoned that they should have premarital sex to see if they truly love a woman. That's a huge misunderstanding of the purpose of sex.

"SEX WAS GIVEN BY GOD TO HELP EXPRESS LOVE, NOT TO CREATE IT."
—DR. MYLES MUNROE

The sexual act of a married couple is a celebration of their love for one another; sex isn't the cause of the relationship. There are three foundations that people build relationships upon:

1. **THE PHYSICAL DIMENSION**—If you build your relationship on the dimension of sex, you are building upon a very narrow foundation. When this happens the relationship falls down when the excitement level drops. A man continues to look for younger and younger replacements, because this type of relationship is all about his sexual satisfaction.

2. **THE SOULISH DIMENSION**—This is a broader foundation because it involves the mind, will, and emotions. You may agree intellectually. You may have strong emotions invested in the relationship. You may have determined objectives with your will. This relationship has a much greater success rate than merely the physical, because it includes the mental and the physical.

3. **THE SPIRITUAL DIMENSION**—If you establish your relationship on a spiritual foundation you are unlimited in relational capacity. The spiritual dimension includes the physical and soulish dimensions. Spiritual agreement is unlimited and includes the mind, will, and emotions. The physical dimension becomes a celebration of the other parts.

HOW CAN A MAN KEEP HIMSELF PURE?

When societies lose the directional markers of purpose, they cast off all restraint. The 1960s sexual revolution ushered in a degrading of America's young people. The idea to remain sexually pure is laughable to some; yet, it is gaining resurgence among the younger generation, especially among young men. It certainly isn't easy with overexposure of sexual content in the media; however, young men are seeing the value of purity for themselves and are attracted to young women who have respected themselves enough to remain pure.

With so much sexual impurity in the world today, how can a young man keep himself pure? For that matter, how can any man keep himself pure?

Solomon, a man who knew women far better than most, gives us guidance:

- Pay attention to wisdom (Proverbs 7:1–5).
- Keep your distance from seductive women (Proverbs 7:6–8).
- Don't give an ear to seductive words (Proverbs 7:5).
- Go home after work (Proverbs 7:9).
- Bounce your eye from the brazen look (Proverbs 7:13).
- Know the difference between lust and love (Proverbs 7:18).
- Honor another man's wife (Proverbs 7:19).
- Don't be persuaded (Proverbs 7:21).
- Understand that impurity is a trap (Proverbs 7:22).
- An adulterous woman will embarrass you (Proverbs 7:23).
- An adulterous woman will escort you to your death (Proverbs 7:27).

Keeping yourself pure is not going to be easy, but there is a purpose for doing so. Few people get to experience the incredible rewards of a relationship that has endured through the years, with the layers and layers of intimacy that dig deep into the depth of a passionate love.

The sexual relationship of a husband and wife becomes an intimate celebration of their lives. It is so much more powerful to have a celebration with your wife than a tryst with a whore.

Lust is an angry and hostile relationship with a stranger who has entangled herself with countless other men; but love is a passionate celebration of purity and commitment between two people who have dedicated themselves to the Lord and to each other.

Men, keep yourself pure, and there will be a day when you realize what I am talking about.

THE GALLANT MAN IS PROTECTIVE

It is part of God's original intent for you to protect what He has placed underneath your care—namely, your wife and children.

God instructed Adam to care for the Garden. Adam was put in the position to have dominion over his home. It has always been the man's responsibility to protect his home. Adam had authority over all the animals in Eden, including creeping things. When Satan entered the serpent, Adam had the authority to shut the serpent up. He should have exercised his authority and stomped on the devil's head.

Build a hedge around your home.

You must protect your environment. That means that you should filter what you allow to enter your home. Whether it is through the front door, the cable or satellite dish, or the Internet, you have the authority to protect your home.

Marriage has a nemesis—an enemy—a scheming and divisive force that wants to destroy your relationship with your wife.

Satan contests everything from God. He can't stand the thought of agreement, truth, and harmony, so he'll do anything that he can to break up your marriage.

Satan also knows that *"where two agree on earth as touching anything, the Spirit of God is in the midst of them"* (Matthew 18:19–20, author's paraphrase). He wants to be the third-party in your relationship. He wants to intertwine his schemes into your marriage through jealousy, envy, manipulation, greed, pride, harsh words, anger, and sexual sin.

The destruction of every marriage can be traced to the devil's destructive third voice. Here are the keys to building a hedge of protection around your marriage:

1. **CREATE AND PROTECT THE ATMOSPHERE OF YOUR HOME.**
   Don't allow strife to enter in. Where there is strife, there is every evil work. **Don't underestimate the destructive power of strife.**

   It's a given that music creates an atmosphere. In much the same way, television can create an atmosphere by bringing complete strangers and strange ideas into your home. Make sure that you aren't introducing strife into your environment through "entertainment." Murder and adultery is not the kind of entertainment you should have in your home.

   You would never invite your neighbors to come into your home and share their intimate details or have sexual relations in front of you.

2. **ATTEND A CHURCH THAT SUPPORTS PROPER RELATIONSHIPS.**

A church that promotes the ideas of authentic manhood, honors and respects women, and provides safe and nurturing programs to help raise your children in the instruction of God's Word is essential.

Has the fruit of your pastor's teaching produced a healthy family in his home? Does the leadership in your church model a strong family life? The Bible qualifies ministerial leadership. If a leader cannot be faithful to his own marriage, what makes you think he will honor yours?

Besides just attending church, you should also regularly pray and discuss God's Word with your wife. Communicate with her, especially over your tithes and offerings. Worship together. Make room for the gifts of the Spirit to work in your home. The third voice in your marriage should be the Spirit of God. He should always have an open invitation to counsel you and remind you of your vows.

3. **KEEP YOUR RELATIONS CONFIDENTIAL.**

Don't discuss private issues with anyone outside of your relationship. It's inappropriate to reveal intimacies. No locker room talk. You're not in junior high. Keep your marriage bed holy.

4. **BE GRATEFUL FOR YOUR WIFE.**

Express your gratitude for the woman and mother that your wife is. She's an individual who has willingly connected to your dreams and goals in life. Studies overwhelmingly reveal that when a husband helps his wife around the house a couple has more intimacy. Guys, it's worth the effort.

5. **SPEAK WORDS OF AFFIRMATION TO HER.**
   She must hear from you. Faith comes from hearing. Speak words that build her up, strengthen and encourage her. Speak kind and comforting words. Your words sanctify her. Learn how to communicate with your wife. Learn what she needs to hear from you. In times of trouble, don't reveal your fears and insecurities! You must show yourself as a man. She will draw strength from you.

6. **CONTINUE TO COURT HER.**
   Date your wife as if you were in the continual pursuit of her. Open doors for her. Stand up, embrace, and greet her when she enters into your world, such as when she visits you at the office or at work. She should be the only woman that you "look" at.

Keep the spark in your marriage alive by making it a practice to take your wife out on dates.

If you are going out on a date, shower, groom, and dress appropriately for it. Court your wife by putting effort into a date with her. Make it an *intentional date*; meaning, don't get in the car and say, "Where do you want to go?" Plan ahead as if you were courting her. A princess likes to be rescued. Your date night will rescue her from the mundane work of motherhood.

Kay and I have a standing date night. Every Friday night we go out to dinner or to a movie. In fact, most of our Fridays are reserved as date *days*. It is a thrill to go on old-fashioned dates with my wife.

Guys, keep the thrill of dating in your marriage. It's better for you in the long run. It's also cheaper to date your wife than to have a girlfriend. Don't be fooled by an adulterous woman—she's not all that—she isn't the wife of your youth.

RAISE UP YOUR CHILDREN

One of the primary functions of the original intent of man is to be a father. We are plagued in our nation with absentee fatherhood. This is a scourge on society. Less than 50 percent of America's children are being raised with a father in the household.

I know a Fivestarman entrepreneur who had a child from a one-night encounter. At the time, he was not living as a Christian, but he turned his life back to Christ and dedicated himself to live honorably. Although he did not marry the stranger with whom he fathered a child, he committed to be in his daughter's life, believing that one day she would live in his home.

I suggested to him that he honor the mother of his child, regardless of the unique and contentious circumstances. He dedicated himself not to speak evil of her and to treat her with respect so that his child would see his conduct toward her. I also recommended that he prepare a room in his house for his daughter.

He had a room decorated and furnished for his little girl. At first, the girl would not have much to do with him, but as she is getting older, the bond between them has become wonderful. She desires to be with him. She wants to live under his roof. She recognizes the difference in the atmospheres of her two homes; she desires the peace and protection of her father's home.

THE FATHER'S HEART

> *"Look, I am sending you the prophet Elijah before the great and dreadful day of the Lord arrives. His preaching will turn the hearts of fathers* to their children, and the hearts of the children to their fathers.* Otherwise I will come and strike the land with a curse"* (Malachi 4:5–6, NLT; [*Hebrew]).

The father's heart must be turned to the child before the child's heart responds to his direction. A man bonds with his children differently than a woman does. The mother is a nurturer, while the father is a protector. The mother caresses, while the father disciplines. The mother's love is expressed through tears, while the father's love is expressed through laughter. When children need comfort, they run to their mother. When children need cash, they run to their father.

Don't be jealous of the way your children react to their mother. As they get older, their relationship will grow deeper and closer toward you. There will be a fundamental shift when they become young adults. Their respect for you will grow immensely. Your primary responsibility is not to become their best friend, but to be their father.

A FATHER GIVES

"For God so loved the world that he gave . . . " (John 3:16).

The love of the Father is to give. Love is expressed in giving out of one's self. A father is sacrificial in his giving toward his children. When my oldest daughter turned sixteen, I began to think about how many summers she had left in my household. My other two children were close behind her at fourteen and ten years old. I decided to sell my golf clubs in order to spend more time with them while they were growing up. It was a small investment of a few years. I did not start playing golf again until my children pooled their resources together and purchased me a new set of clubs. They apparently needed more time with dad.

There may be something that you can do to be adventurous together with your children while they are growing up. My youngest daughter loves to play golf and plays on her high school golf team.

Some fathers try to "gift" their way through a relationship. Although children love this at first, they begin to despise the gifts because they do not adequately represent his love over time.

You are the gift. As a father, you must realize that your presence is a gift to your child.

A FATHER GUIDES

Never discipline whom you've not *discipled*.

You may have had this happen to you as a boy. Your curiosity and sense of adventure got you into a mess. Then you got into terrible trouble because you didn't know that what you did was wrong, dumb, or foolish.

A few years ago, I became frustrated at one of my children because they did something blatantly foolish. I couldn't believe it. I wanted to explode in my anger, but the Holy Spirit began to instruct me saying, "Neil, did you ever instruct your child about this? When did you teach a principle concerning this? Never discipline whom you've not discipled."

I have a responsibility to teach my children. This is not something I can pawn off on others and expect the results that I want. I can't shrug off this duty. Yes, I can employ a school teacher and entrust my children to be raised in a church, but it is my calling to train them in the way they are to go.

Did you know that Abraham was chosen to be in covenant with God because of his teaching ability?

That's right. God chose him because, *"He will direct his children and his household after him to keep the way of the LORD by doing what is right and just, so that the LORD will bring about for Abraham what he has promised"* (Genesis 18:19).

God actually assigned His covenant blessing to Abraham because Abraham could be trusted to teach.

Children are insatiable learners. If we do not teach them, they will get their wisdom from someone else. Unfortunately, they often will go to the unknowing for knowledge. The knowledge that children learn from the world or from their friends is often the knowledge of wrongdoing and evil. It can be sinful and wicked. Don't delegate your responsibility to others.

Abraham's teaching ability would ensure God's promises. God said, *"I will bring about for Abraham what I have promised."*

If you want to ensure that your children do not depart from the way of God, you must teach them.

Here is the simple, three-step strategy I use to teach:

1. **PRECEPT**—A precept is an established authority. It is immovable, eternal, foundational truth. When you read the Word of God, look for precepts. When you start with a precept, your teaching is based upon foundational truth and authority. It isn't because you say so, but because it is established. An example of a precept is, "Do not muzzle the ox while he is treading the grain." This is an agrarian and ethical treatment rule to allow an ox to graze while he is working.

2. **PRINCIPLE**—A principle is the universal truth and application of a precept. The principle should direct my behavior, belief system, and conduct. Our example about the ox helps us understand that we should employ ethical treatment of an animal that is under our care or in use for our labor.

3. **PRACTICE**—Practice is taking the precept, converting it to a principle, and applying it to my life. I do not have an

ox, so is this precept relevant to me? It might not seem so, but the apostle Paul used this example to teach that ministers of the gospel should receive their financial salaries from ministering the gospel.

We are created with a deep desire to learn and to receive knowledge. We should always look to expand our minds, to learn, and to think. As men, we don't want to participate in useless exercises based on theory. We want to know what works. Call it street smarts or common sense, but men want practical, real-life applications. Your children are no different. They need real-world knowledge, too. Your children need to know how to make and invest money. They need to know what to do if the car breaks down or they have an accident.

Practically speaking, I teach my children as we go through life, when we're driving, playing golf, eating, etc. Don't try to over-structure your teaching time with them. Teach as you do life together. A lot of fathers attempt to sit down with their family basically copying the format of a church service; it really doesn't work very well.

One thing that I do with my family that I would suggest for any home is to have communion together when you are facing a difficult situation, or especially when you are writing out your tithe check. It's an amazing experience when you invoke God's blessing upon your home through communion.

A FATHER GUARDS

"Discipline your son, for in that there is hope; do not be a willing party to his death" (Proverbs 19:18).

Fathers are responsible to discipline their children. Don't pawn this off on your wife. Discipline from you is a protective measure. You are not punishing your children, but protecting them.

Without discipline you are willingly surrendering your child to other forces to control his or her behavior. How many times have you heard about a misguided father who constantly bails out his child from misbehavior or criminal activity?

When you fail to discipline your child you are surrendering him or her to the correction of society. That's a harsh reality because the world has no mercy.

David commented on falling into the hands of the judgment of man and said, *"I am in deep distress. Let me fall into the hands of the LORD, for his mercy is very great; but do not let me fall into the hands of men"* (1 Chronicles 21:11).

Fathers sometimes fail to lead their families because they feel inferior to do so.

A man once told me, "Neil, I just don't feel like I have the moral authority to tell my children what they should do. I was not a good example. I didn't live right. I'm working at it now, but how can I lead them knowing that I did the very things that I tell them not to do?"

We must teach the lessons we've learned from life, even some hard lessons because of our stupidity. We must lead our children to avoid foolishness and seek wisdom. Discipline your children. Don't be a co-conspirator in their destruction. Here are some practical steps:

YOU MUST STAY IN CONTROL OF YOUR OWN EMOTIONS IN ORDER TO GUIDE THE EMOTIONS OF YOUR CHILD.

Some parents don't discipline until they've reached a boiling point. When they've "had enough," they burst into an uncontrollable rage. Don't do that. *Calmly* approach the discipline.

THE PURPOSE OF DISCIPLINE IS TO CHANGE INAPPROPRIATE BEHAVIOR AND TO GIVE THE CHILD THE ABILITY TO DISCERN BETWEEN RIGHT AND WRONG.

Be very *specific* as to why you are disciplining your children. They must know what they did wrong.

ESTABLISH DISCIPLINE EARLY IN LIFE SO YOU WON'T HAVE TO USE IT AS MUCH LATER.

You will already have established their respect for you.

DON'T COUNT TO THREE.

Parents have a ridiculous habit of counting to three (or five or ten) before they will discipline. This trains the child to think that they can delay their obedience. Teach your child to obey your words *immediately*. If you were crossing a road and a car was screaming toward your child, you wouldn't have time to count to three. Teach your child to obey immediately.

MATCH THE PUNISHMENT TO THE OFFENSE.

Make certain that you don't exaggerate the punishment. Don't ground your child *"for life."*

TEACH YOUR CHILD THAT IT IS BETTER TO LIVE UNDER THE BLESSINGS OF YOUR HAND THAN THE CURSE.

Always connect disobedience with lack, and obedience with supply. If your child is believing for something—a new cell phone, clothes, etc.—don't remove their daily *needs*, but delay their *wants* to discipline them.

SET THE TONE EARLY IN LIFE SO YOU WON'T HAVE TO DEAL WITH REBELLION AS THEY GET OLDER.

Before he reaches rebellious actions, a child will speak disrespectfully or cuttingly toward you or their mother. (In most cases they start with their mother.) If you stop them at the level of *words*, you can avoid rebellion in *action*.

DON'T BE INTIMIDATED BY YOUR CHILD.

Don't let your child manipulate or threaten you. Stay in control.

Society has turned against physical punishment. There are plenty of debates on the issue. There is so much confusion on the matter. I believe in spanking a child if it is necessary. My wife and I spanked our children when they were young to establish obedience to our words.

Father, you must watch over your words to perform them. If you don't value what you say, neither will your family. If they know that you *mean* what you say, they will *do* what you say. By the way, if they know that you will honor what you command, they also will learn to value your words when you say, "I love you."

BEST-DRESSED MAN

> *"So Pharaoh sent for Joseph, and he was quickly brought from the dungeon. When he had shaved and changed his clothes, he came before Pharaoh"* (Genesis 41:14).

Joseph had a spiritual gift that allowed him to interpret dreams. Pharaoh needed a dream to be interpreted. The gift within Joseph invited him into the presence of the leader of the world. Falsely accused, Joseph had spent years in the prison dungeon. Suddenly he was summoned into the highest court of authority.

Before he went into that room, Joseph shaved and dressed appropriately for the meeting.

A gallant man is well groomed and dresses appropriately for every occasion.

As American men, we have become very sloppy in our dress. We should rethink it. Evidence overwhelmingly supports that a well-dressed person achieves success in every endeavor more effectively than a person who is dressed sloppily.

Being appropriately dressed helps give you the boost of confidence you need to participate in a meeting or an event.

As I have mentioned, I like golf. When I play golf, I dress for the occasion. At times I've had a few guys mock me because I dress in a more traditional, upscale manner for the golf course; however, I respect the game and I play a better round of golf when I dress for it. I have also noticed that when we play a second time, the person who previously mocked me, will usually step up his dress knowing how I will be dressed for the round. I believe my attire is appreciated and respected.

LESSONS TO DRESS APPROPRIATELY:

YOUR PRESENTATION IS IMPORTANT.
Men often quote, *"Man looks at the outward appearance but the LORD looks at the heart"* (1 Samuel 16:7). Well, that's true, but here on Earth, you live with man. Man looks on the outward appearance.

STEP UP YOUR GAME.
Dressing appropriately portrays you as a person of influence and authority. Know what the proper dress is for an occasion, and dress one notch above the rest in the room. This will immediately establish you as the "go-to" guy.

DON'T GET STUCK.
Don't get nostalgic concerning how you dress. You look silly wearing outdated clothing or clothes that aren't culturally relevant. For an example, don't wear Ralph Lauren Polo clothes designed for the bay or the Hamptons out to west Texas. Texans have appropriate attire for the ranch. Geography plays a huge role in what is proper. People dress primarily for function and climate. Plan accordingly.

DON'T UNDER-DRESS OR OVER-DRESS FOR THE OCCASION.

Either one is embarrassing. It is never wrong to ask what the expected attire is.

FOCUS ON DETAILS.

How to tie a necktie is a lesson that every young man should learn. Wearing the right color socks can make or break you. The proper shoes are also a fine detail that should not be overlooked.

It is manly to dress appropriately. If you study history you will find that man has always valued his appearance. You may scoff at this, but you know that it's true. Shake off your embarrassment, step it up, and dress appropriately.

The same is true for grooming. Guys, after forty years of age, you'll need to groom your ear hairs and tweak your eyebrows. Don't get stuck with a haircut that doesn't fit your head or your time. Update your look. Learning to shave properly is another skill that every young man should have. Obviously, showering every day should go without saying, but I am speaking to men. If your Daddy didn't tell you, then let me emphasize it. Men, you must shower every day

PASSION FOUR

FAITHFUL IN CHARACTER

PROLOGUE

It was one of the most amazing experiences a young man could have. While on vacation in Colorado, Joseph decided to sleep under the stars. He took his sleeping bag, a flashlight, and his thermal underwear and trekked out to find a clearing. He found the best spot imaginable. The sunset was casting magical shadows on Grand Mesa. A young man, Joseph was so excited, yet he also felt a sense of destiny in his adventure. He had a churning feeling deep within him, almost like a calling coming from his belly. It was a strange feeling.

After spending a few hours getting his campsite prepared for the night, he hiked a full circle around it to explore his new territory. Then he returned to his spot, got settled into the bag, and looked up into the sky. His eyes began to focus on the details of the stars, which became clearer and clearer. It was simply awesome.

That's when it happened.

As his eyes seemed to have a limitless potential to see the universe, Joseph began to dream a dream while he was still awake. It seemed so real; yet he knew it was symbolic.

Joseph was standing in front of a crowd. Their eyes were fixated upon him, and every word he said was recorded. He was a leader. The faces in the crowd looked upon him with respect and a mystical admiration. He saw himself dressed very well, looking distinguished in his appearance. His voice was soothing and confident. It had a rhythmic cadence that made his words seem to dance through the air and into the ears of his listeners.

As he was speaking, he looked to his left and saw a few people with smirks on their faces and eyes that seemed to hold judgment. Their hands were stuffed in their pockets, as if they were holding something. Their posture was defiant. Joseph knew that he had enemies.

Joseph tossed in his sleeping bag and curled up even more to try to recover the body heat that had escaped into the cool night air. Then the dream went into another stage.

His wife and his children gathered into the family room of their home, which was a very nice estate. His cars were lined up in the garage like stallions waiting their turn to run. The grand house was filled with treasures, mementos of his successful life. As he walked into the room, his children jumped to their feet to hug him, his wife embraced him with compassionate love. Although he knew these people were his family, he couldn't see the details of their identity. He just knew that it was wonderful.

Now the cold was starting to work against him. Joseph thought that he might have to return to the cabin, but he didn't want to leave the theater of his dream. He knew that he was getting a glimpse into his future. He needed it. He remembered that he had brought a couple of HeatMax hand warmers. He forced himself back into his sleeping bag, the warmers seeming to work perfectly. Within minutes he was cozy. That allowed him to return to the dream.

The scene had changed again. This time he was in his spacious corner office when several men burst in to meet him, his assistant frantically trying to stop them. They were his partners, men with whom he had built the company. Their faces told the story. They were there for blood.

Something was terribly wrong, and they had obviously judged Joseph as the culprit. As Joseph stood up to greet them, attempting to calm their aggression, he noticed someone. It was the same group of enemies that he had seen earlier in the crowd, in the first scene of the dream. Yet, they weren't really there. They were standing behind his partners, constantly whispering. He couldn't really hear what they were saying, but then he realized that they were feeding lies and slander to his friends.

"What's in the closet, Joseph?" Ted asked with a gesture toward the doors.

Tom, another but lesser partner, mused, "Yeah, what do you keep in there? We want to know. We think that you've been stealing from us, keeping things from us. What's in there?"

As Joseph walked toward the closet, he realized that he was about to open himself up in ways that he never had before. When he revealed the secret, his friends, family, and business partners would never look at him the same.

As he slowly, opened the door, he glanced back and said, "Guys, I've always operated with the highest level of integrity. I have conducted my business with you honestly, and we've succeeded like few have. What I am about to show you is the secret to my success."

The hand warmers had faded into a dull lukewarmness. He squeezed his hands hoping to get more out of them. It was too late. The cold was just too much, the dream was gone, and Joseph had to get back to the cabin.

As he walked back, he looked up into the expanse of the sky and said, "God, I know the secret."

FAITHFUL IN CHARACTER

"The man of integrity walks securely, but he who takes crooked paths will be found out" (Proverbs 10:9).

The Fivestarman is faithful in his character. He is authentic. He is true to the original intent. He is ethical in his business. He is a principled man. He is a spiritual man, but he's not religious. He wants a practical relationship with God, not a pious one.

This is the passion that separates the authentic man from the façade, the player. Don't underestimate the importance of this passion because it will make you or break you. You won't get away with being inconsistent and fake. This is the secret to success.

The movie *The Godfather* has a memorable exchange in it that goes like this:

Fontane: A month ago he bought the rights to this book, a bestseller. The main character is a guy just like me. I wouldn't even have to act, just be myself. Oh, Godfather, I don't know what to do. I don't know what to do. . . .
[*All of a sudden, Don Corleone rises from his chair and gives Fontane a savage shake.*]

Corleone: YOU CAN ACT LIKE A MAN!
[*He gives Fontane a quick slap.*]
What's the matter with you?! Is this what you've become, a Hollywood finocchio who cries like a woman? "Oh, what do I do? What

do I do?" What is that nonsense? Ridiculous! [*The Don's unexpected mimicry makes Hagen and even Fontane laugh.*]

Corleone: Tell me, do you spend time with your family?

Fontane: Sure I do.

Corleone: Good, because a man who doesn't spend time with his family can never be a real man.

Some men compartmentalize their lives—business, family, and faith all have their own world, and they don't intertwine. The Godfather compartmentalizes what manhood is, *"It's not personal; it's business."*

That kind of thinking is delusional.

A man's life can't be divided into segments—the word *integrity* means **undivided**. It means *wholeness* or *fullness*.

As a man, you were created with integrity. God created you in His image. When Adam sinned against his Creator, he perverted his integrity. Adam compromised his walk with God, and mankind became aware of alternate paths—all of which are a lie.

GOD RELATES TO MAN IN THE WALK

Adam walked with God in the cool of the day (Genesis 3:8).

Enoch walked with God and he was no more for God took him (Genesis 5:24).

Noah walked with God (Genesis 6:9).

Abraham walked with God to a place where he didn't know where he was going (Hebrews 11:8).

Moses walked with God on the Holy Mountain (Exodus 19:3).

David walked with God in the valley of the shadow of death (Psalm 23:4).

Jesus, God with us, walked with His disciples, relating to them on a practical level.

> *"If the* LORD *delights in a man's way, he makes his steps firm"* *(Psalm 37:23).*

Jesus gave us an outline to speak with God the Father. Let me break it down in a simple form, so that as you walk, you can talk with God:

FATHER—Initiate the conversation. *"God"* is really a generic term. I prefer to call on God as Father, which is the most intimate and respectful name to use.

HALLOWED BE YOUR NAME—Remember that our Father is holy. Practice the protocol of addressing Him in the name of Jesus. The name of Jesus is like the key that unlocks the door of Heaven. In fact, it is the only key. No other name is given to men for salvation, so use the name of Jesus to speak with the Father.

YOUR KINGDOM COME—Ask the Father to exercise His ways and principles in your life. When you ask the Father in faith to do His will on the Earth, it gives Him a license to intervene in your world.

GIVE US EACH DAY OUR DAILY BREAD—Ask God to help you be successful today in meeting your needs, providing for your family, and financing your purpose.

FORGIVE US OUR SINS—Ask God to forgive you for your shortcomings.

FOR WE ALSO FORGIVE EVERYONE WHO SINS AGAINST US—Make sure that you have released anyone who has sinned against you. When you do, you cancel out the effect of that sin in your life. Don't allow a bitter root to grow in your heart.

LEAD US NOT INTO TEMPTATION—Ask God to lead you. Doing so means that you will be guided into righteousness. James 1:13 assures us that God does not tempt us with evil; therefore, know that your Father's leading is the path of righteousness.

MAN RELATES TO GOD IN HIS DAILY WALK

You can't compartmentalize your faithfulness into just attending church every few Sundays. **Your walk with God must be a daily commute.**

If a man is trying to get all of his spiritual encouragement from attending church, he is going to be a spiritually weak and anemic man.

For the most part, churches are designed for women, and men relate to them as if they were visiting an elderly aunt's outdated home filled with floral patterned couches, fake flowers, pastel colors, and the smell of mothballs. When they do attend church, the worship service is usually poorly designed for men. It caters to women with songs that are emotive and quiet. The prayers are so powerless that you must pinch yourself to keep from falling asleep. An effeminate intellectual who is more interested in showing off his vocabulary than actually saying anything of substance usually delivers the sermon. The service typically ends with a limp-wristed plea to become "nicer and better citizens of the world," a charge that survives in the hearers' minds until they shake the hand of the parson as they leave.

You may think that I'm being sacrilegious, but there isn't an ounce of this formula for church services found in the Bible. My purpose in writing this book is not to instruct churches and ministers on how to design their services for effective communication. There are plenty of new and creative seminars that address those issues. My purpose is to address men and show them how they can have a daily, practical, vibrant walk with God.

Thankfully, more and more churches are discovering how important it is to effectively communicate to men. They are redesigning their facilities to be more practical, less austere, and more inviting. Many are replacing their feminine décor with earth tones and structurally strong elements, such as wood and rock.

It makes sense to focus on men. Men are the gateway to the family. A biblical example of this is Cornelius in Acts 10.

Cornelius was a Roman Centurion, a righteous and God-fearing man. He was the epitome of a Fivestarman. Following a very interesting visitation of angels, Cornelius sent for Peter to come to his home. The invitation was confirmed to Peter through a vision and a Word of Knowledge from the Holy Spirit, *"Three men are waiting for you to take you with them, don't hesitate to go."*

When Peter entered the home of the Gentile Cornelius, he began to speak about the Good News of Jesus. Not only did Cornelius convert and follow Christ, but his family also followed his lead.

In the book, ***Why Men Hate Going to Church,*** *(Thomas Nelson Publishing, Inc., Nashville, TN, © 2005)* David Murrow said, "When a mother comes to faith in Christ, the rest of her family follows 17 percent of the time. But when a father comes to faith in Christ, the rest of the family follows 93 percent of the time."

The fact is that Dad is destiny. If the father steps up to take the lead, his family will follow. We constantly see this demonstrated in the negative in our society; but we can turn this around when men MAN UP!

Interestingly, as far as the biblical record, Cornelius is the first Gentile who converted to Christianity. The Jewish believers with

Peter recognized that Cornelius had received the evidence of the Holy Spirit, so they reasoned that the Gentiles must be accepted in the wonderful plan of God's redemptive work.

LEAD YOUR FAMILY IN FAITH

The authentic man is a man who leads his family in faith. The strength of his personal relationship with God is an inspiration to his wife and children to carry on in the face of trials and temptations. Although he is not perfect, the life that he leads demonstrates that the deepest desire of his heart is to follow God and accomplish his unique purpose.

HAVE A PERSONAL WALK WITH GOD.

Your family will see the credibility of your faith through your consistent relationship with your Father. The greatest compliment will be when you hear you children say, "I will serve the God of my father."

WATCH OVER YOUR WORDS.

Your words are incredibly important to your family. They must see that you value your words when you speak. Also, let them overhear you praying. This isn't for show; it's for discipleship. Jesus invited His disciples to pray with Him, even though they fell asleep and were weak in the flesh.

"The words of a righteous man are a well of life"
(Proverbs 10:11, author's paraphrase).

LET THEM SEE YOU READING THE BIBLE.

Don't be embarrassed to let them know that you read the Word of God. When you quote the Word, don't use it as a club. Speak kind and comforting words. Speak words that encourage, build up, and inspire. Don't get caught up in quoting the references of the Bible; it sounds contrived. Let the Word flow naturally from your lips, even paraphrasing it in your language, so long as you don't misspeak the meaning.

WHEN FACING CHALLENGES, INVITE THEM TO JOIN IN ON YOUR FAITH WALK THROUGH IT.

Whether financially or physically, this will equip them and help them develop their own faith for action in their lives.

RELATE TO YOUR KIDS NOT ONLY AS YOUR CHILDREN, BUT ALSO AS BROTHERS AND SISTERS IN CHRIST.

HAVE COMMUNION TOGETHER OVER YOUR TITHES AND OFFERINGS.

This will connect your family to the celebration of provision and giving.

LET THEM SEE YOUR STRENGTH, BUT LET THEM ALSO SEE YOUR SUBMISSION.

God's Word must reign as the authority of your life.

To be an authentic man, you must live under the principles of God's Word. Knowing how God has ordered creation is extremely important for applying His principles in your life and letting them benefit your family.

WHEN A MAN FALLS

So what if you fail? What do you do? Do you give up?

No, emphatically. NO!

> *"Though a righteous man falls seven times, he rises again, but the wicked are brought down by calamity" (Proverbs 24:16).*

All men fail. The righteous get back up. I read a lot of biographies, and I have yet to find a story that didn't include failures. In fact, the story **IS** the failure and how the man got back up to win and become successful. Most successful men will tell you more about their failures than they do their successes. It's the thrill of winning out over failure that makes them proud.

If you have failed, so what?

You're in good company—that is if you get back up. Only losers stay down.

> *"I write this to you so that you will not sin. But if anybody does sin, we have one who speaks to the Father in our defense—Jesus Christ, the Righteous One" (1 John 2:1).*

Thank God we have an Advocate with the Father! So don't give up. Get up and go after it. I'm certainly not suggesting that you play games with this. Don't use grace as a license to keep sinning. That's foolish and perverted thinking. No, I'm talking about the man of integrity who succumbs to temptation in whatever capacity but deals with it properly and takes steps to be victorious in his life. That's integrity. Being a man of integrity is being able to recalibrate your life to the standard of excellence.

MAKE THE DECISION

I'm going to challenge you to think this out. The decision to be a faithful man is one you must make personally. Too often we have allowed ourselves the excuse that only God can work His will in our lives. Without taking anything away from God's omnipotence, He can't save you without your consent. God is not willing that any should perish; yet there are millions who do. They perish because they decide not to submit their egotistical thinking to the Lordship of Christ.

We need men who will make the quality decision to man up and be decisive in their faithfulness.

In the fall of 1983, I was working in a coal mine in Oklahoma. I had faced some very humiliating circumstances and was desperately trying to get a handle on my life. I was alone and confused. At the invitation of a friend, I began to attend a local church. After a few services the pastor walked from the platform to where I was sitting. He sat down beside me and asked, "Neil, are you ready to make a decision to accept Christ?"

"I will, but right now I'm trying to clean up a few things in my life," I replied.

"You'll never be able to do that. That's what Christ does. You simply need to make a decision," he suggested.

At that moment, I got up with him, walked the aisle to kneel down at the steps of an altar, and followed his leading to pray a simple prayer.

To the disappointment of the regular attendees, I showed no emotion. I'm sure that many of them assumed I didn't really get saved. When I left that church and returned to my home, I lifted my hands and thanked God for his mercy to save me.

Yes, I got saved that day, but it was a quality decision that I made, not an emotional one.

My salvation is much like my marriage. I made a quality decision to accept Christ, and I made a quality decision to marry my wife. To be sure, I have wonderful emotional feelings about both, but at times when those feelings are not present, I still will not change my mind on either.

Faithfulness is expressing your belief in God through your conduct and behavior.

Being a faithful man is being a reliable, consistent, steadfast, determined, and trustworthy person. It means that you mean what you say, and say what you mean.

The Fivestarman is faithful in his relationships, both with God and man.

USE CAUTION IN RELATIONSHIPS

You must be careful how you relate to others. People who become too familiar with you may become contemptuous. They may take advantage of you.

Job found out how quickly friends could become contemptuous. While he was lying on his sick bed, they lectured him. Their words were resentful and slanderous against God. Even Job's wife cursed God.

You must guard yourself from poor relationships. The older I get, the more I realize how important the selection of friends is. There are some people you must avoid and some relationships you must guard against:

- Don't trust someone who doesn't respect your relationship with God (Psalm 14:1).
- Don't trust someone who mocks God (Proverbs 19:3).
- Don't trust someone who creates his own religion. Some men design their own belief systems to fit their lifestyles (Proverbs 28:26).
- Don't trust someone who is always in contention with another person (Proverbs 18:6).
- Don't trust someone who continues to repeat the same mistakes over and over (Proverbs 26:11).
- Don't trust someone who bursts out in tantrums and rages to get his way (Proverbs 27:3).

CHARACTERISTICS OF A FAITHFUL MAN

A FAITHFUL MAN HAS CLARITY OF VISION.

You are able to focus on details; yet at the same time, you're able to see long range. Faithful men are able to discern things that others can't see. They see what's ahead and are able to plan accordingly.

A few years ago, I began to see troubling signs in the economy. I felt a very clear warning to change the way that I managed my money. I had a strong urgency to get out of debt. As I prepared to do so and set my course, the housing bubble burst. I can honestly say that if I hadn't heeded the warning, I could have gone bankrupt.

A faithful man is able to prepare for the worst of situations by seeing ahead of coming events. Noah was warned about the flood, so he built an ark to save his family.

A FAITHFUL MAN SPEAKS CLEARLY.

Your words matter more than you may think. The Bible says that your words have the authority of life and death within them. A faithful man should speak truthfully. He should speak clearly, making the most of every opportunity. Your words should be precise, accurate, and appropriate for each moment.

A FAITHFUL MAN MUST HAVE CLEAN HANDS.

A faithful man makes sure that his hands are not misused in business or in personal affairs. You've heard the saying, "Keep your hands clean." This statement is not concerned with the dirt of work, but the corruption of business. Make sure that you're conducting your business with integrity.

A FAITHFUL MAN IS CREATIVE AND PRODUCTIVE.

Don't devise schemes that are dishonest. Use your talents wisely, investing your energy toward noble purposes. I've known men who have devised all kinds of moneymaking ventures that are nothing more than Ponzi schemes. I've often thought that if they would use half of their creativity and effort to do something useful, they would not only be productive, but they would also prosper in the process.

A FAITHFUL MAN AVOIDS EVIL.

Don't go where you would never take you wife or mother. Don't excuse yourself by saying, "Well, it's business. I have to do it. I have to entertain clients." I've seen men throw away their integrity by going to the bar or strip club for the sake of "entertaining clients." If you have to bribe your clients, then you need to rethink your product.

A FAITHFUL MAN DOES NOT GOSSIP.

You should avoid gossip like the plague. Don't belittle or speak a rumor about anyone. If you spread lies or tell stories so that you can curry favor with someone, you're gossiping. Don't do it. Avoid the conversation all together. If someone begins to speak about a situation that is none of your business or outside of your authority, simply excuse yourself from the room.

A FAITHFUL MAN OVERLOOKS AN INSULT.

There will always be people who speak negatively about you. There will be people who are jealous and envious of you. Don't react. Ignore them. If you start chasing after and defending yourself against every insult, you won't have time to do anything else.

A FAITHFUL MAN IS PRUDENT.

You don't hear much about prudence, but it is an art form. If you are prudent you will take care of your possessions. Solomon said, *"The wise [prudent] have wealth and luxury, but fools spend whatever they get"* (Proverbs 21:20, NLT). A faithful man keeps his house in order and his car clean and well maintained. You can't get a new car just because your ashtray is full. Take good care of your possessions.

A FAITHFUL MAN IS DISCIPLINED.

You must stay in control of your personal discipline. Watch how you eat, and maintain your health. Make sure that you stay away from any addictions, be they food, alcohol, drugs, or even caffeine. A faithful man controls his appetites.

A FAITHFUL MAN MANAGES HIS MONEY.

Money is a means to an end. Don't chase after money for the accumulation of it. It will sprout wings and fly away. If you'll give each dollar an assignment, you'll raise its value to fulfill your purpose. Spend less than you make, and you'll see your money grow and grow.

A FAITHFUL MAN IS DILIGENT.

Don't be slack in your work. Work as if you're working directly for the Lord, as if He is paying your wages. Be faithful no matter who sees what you do. This will bring you prosperity and promotion. Promotion does not come from man, but it is dictated from the Lord.

A FAITHFUL MAN HONORS THE WIFE OF HIS YOUTH.

Don't dishonor your covenant with your wife. I've never seen an adulterous man live a full and complete life. His life is cut short. The Bible says that the Earth trembles under the feet of a married woman who is unloved (Proverbs 30:23). God will avenge your wife, if you abandon her to chase after teenage fantasies.

A FAITHFUL MAN SEEKS WISDOM.

I'm disgusted with reading that men are simple-minded, that we are not readers. That is foolishness. As I said before, leaders are readers. If you are going to be a faithful man you must have an insatiable appetite to read. Reading books enlarges your world. Don't blow this off. It's not manly to be a fool.

A FAITHFUL MAN IS PATIENT.

Don't get in too big of a hurry. Making haste leads to poverty. Pace your success, and expect the results of your work. It won't happen overnight, but if you're consistent and don't become weary in doing good work, you'll see your reward. It will be favorable for you. Anything significant in life will require an investment of time and effort.

A FAITHFUL MAN BUILDS HIS LIFE ON THE WORD OF GOD.

- Reading the Word of God is the energy of life (John 1:4).
- Reading the Word of God renews your mind and keeps it clear of offense (Psalm 119:165).
- Reading the Word of God scrubs your stinking thinking (John 15:3).
- Reading the Word of God protects you from impurity (Psalm 119:9).
- Reading the Word of God instructs you in righteousness (2 Timothy 3:16).
- Reading the Word of God elevates you above your competition (Psalm 119:98).
- Reading the Word of God illuminates your spirit (Psalm 119:130).
- Reading the Word of God makes you happy (John 15:11).
- Reading the Word of God clearly identifies right and wrong (Proverbs 3:7).
- Reading the Word of God makes you wise (Proverbs 2:6).

PASSION FIVE

PHILANTHROPIC CAUSE

PROLOGUE

Robert spins his chair around, propping his feet up on his credenza. His eyes begin to take in the breathtaking view from his corner office. He's sitting in the middle of his dream. He worked hard—very hard—to get to this point in his life. It wasn't easy. He navigated several close calls throughout his career, maneuvering effectively through the dangers of being an entrepreneur. Now, after years of focused energy, it has finally hit him. This is the first time he realizes that he has reached the pinnacle of his dream.

His company is a well-oiled machine. It holds contracts extended as far as he will accept them. His cash flow is well beyond the margin of sustaining his dream. His company reserves would keep them successful long beyond most companies. He paid off all his debt years ago and has built a large portfolio of assets.

Personally, his home is a safe-haven. He and his wife, Hayden, not only enjoy one another, but they are passionately in love and completely devoted to one another in marriage and in partnership. His children are out enjoying early successes in their own right, having the launching pad of their dad's success and the investment of quality education as their foundation. Their dad's risk taking has taught them valuable and lasting lessons through the years. There were lean times. There were also times of plenty. The life-lessons have tempered them with wisdom that will protect them from many foolish mistakes.

Robert's thoughts take an unusual excursion when he gazes at the mountainous horizon. *Now what?* he thinks to himself. *Now that the company and I have reached this place, what am I going to focus on?*

He has too much energy and creativity to just coast. No, he can't do that. He's seen too many of his friends become bored with their companies and take foolish risks, getting off course and shipwrecking everything. Not to mention how their boredom cost them their marriages. Most of his colleagues have committed adultery for the sake of the risks, not for the relationships. *I am not going there,* his thoughts continue to counsel him.

A few minutes later a longtime friend calls. "Bob, I want to have coffee with you," says the voice on the phone. "I have someone I want you to meet."

Robert accepts the invitation immediately. "I can meet you now. Let's say . . . a half an hour?"

After the pleasantries, Robert sits down to talk to his friend Randal and the introduced guest, Phil.

Randal begins the conversation, "Bob, I want you to know what I've been up to since leaving my company. I've been involved with philanthropy. I've been very careful to study different organizations and found that many of them are scams. They take too much off the top for administration. They invest too much on fund raising. Frankly, they're poorly managed, and you get very little for your investment. I've worked way too hard in my life to throw my money out to every Tom, Dick, and Harry who has a 501(c)3. That's why I want to introduce Phil," Randal continues in his no-nonsense style, "and the organization that he leads, ChildHope Network."

Then Phil tells the story of ChildHope, how it was started to rescue children from systemic poverty, not just by giving them bread, but by giving them the education that they need to make a life, by giving the children the dignity of a school uniform, by helping them maintain a healthy lifestyle, and by introducing them to the redemptive work of Christ.

Robert asks a series of questions that would cause most leaders to stump and stammer. Phil is able to answer the questions and also to expound on the concepts themselves. Robert is amazed at the depth of information, and he is completely surprised by the overwhelming integrity of the finances. The thirty minutes that he had blocked for the meeting extends to three hours. Robert begins to get a vision, not only for his company, but also for his life.

Following the meeting, the men schedule a visit to a village in southern Mexico. Robert and Hayden and Randal and his wife, Beth, meet with Phil. After seeing the school, the children standing to greet them in every classroom, Robert is amazed at the efficiency and practical excellence of the school. When he shakes hands with the children, they look him in the eye when they speak. That strikes a cord with Robert. *These guys are training leaders,* he thinks to himself.

"Not only are they learning the basics, they are learning languages and computers, leadership skills and personal responsibility," Phil explains.

Robert and Hayden are amazed. As they return to their private jet, they begin to dream of how they can become involved.

"Now I can understand why God has brought us to this place in life. The entrepreneurial gift has brought me extraordinary profits. We have a great life. We live very well without any guilt, because I have lived my life with integrity and conducted my business that way. But now I can use my gifts and our profits for the greater good of humanity. This will be our legacy," Robert surmises. "This is what everything is for!"

PHILANTHROPIC CAUSE

"IS THERE NOT A CAUSE?"
—KING DAVID

The purpose of life is much more than the accumulation of stuff. God gifts us with the entrepreneurial drive to meet our daily needs, provide for our families, and have the sufficiency to fulfill our purpose. The pursuit of our purpose is the ultimate goal.

You've heard that it's said, "I've never seen a hearse pulling a U-Haul trailer." The Egyptian Pharaohs didn't have enough spiritual insight to know that. They were buried with their treasures only to be robbed by the living. When you die, you will take nothing material with you.

So, what's it all for?

It's about leaving a legacy.

> "[God] has also set eternity in the hearts of men" (Ecclesiastes 3:11).

Most pursuits are meaningless. Every month there is an awards show for the Hollywood crowd, the Nashville bunch, or the New York City elites. They walk the red carpet, hobnob with their peers, and scratch each other's backs—and for what?

For a silly little statue that means nothing in the scheme of things worthwhile. When they receive their sculptured idols, they thank their generic gods, acknowledge their cohorts, and give their two-cents worth of political spin. The awards are not legitimate.

They are bought and paid for by the companies that manage their marionette personalities. Frankly, it's embarrassing.

I wonder if God ever looks down on humanity and says, *"Wow, I just expected more."*

It's easy for us to take potshots at that crowd because their narcissism is so much on display—but shouldn't we also take inventory of our own ambitions as men?

What are we doing this for?

At the end of your seasoned life, when you're surveying your ambitions, what will have mattered? In light of eternity—what matters?

I believe it is the investment that you make in the living that is transferred to the eternal. Only the living are eternal.

> ## "WE'RE ALL GOING TO DIE, AND YOU WANT TO MAKE SURE YOU'VE INVESTED YOUR LIFE WISELY."
> —LEROY LANDHUIS

A pastor friend of mine had a dream of building a new facility to minister exclusively to children, the next generation. It was an admirable project, yet he struggled with communicating that dream to his congregants. After he failed to raise the money, he was disgusted when he heard that one of his members had invested $40,000 to save an oak tree that had been damaged. My friend exclaimed, "The man invested that money in a tree! He could have invested it in children!"

By the way, the oak tree died. It's nothing but a stump.

That man did exactly what most people are doing, they're investing into what will rot!

> *"Do not store up for yourselves treasures on earth, where*
> *moth and rust destroy, and where thieves break in and steal"*
> *(Matthew 6:19).*

The philanthropic cause of a man is the deep desire to do something of significance. To live beyond one's self is the desire of the authentic man. The word *philanthropic* means the active effort to better humanity.

When you draw upon this deep passion of man, you will discover that your purpose to live for the sake of others taps you into a creativity and spiritual consciousness that will not be revealed in any other way. Most men never experience this kind of spiritual depth, because they're too busy living for themselves or being tripped up in the silly little snares that men fall into.

In his book, *The Richest Man in Town: The Twelve Commandments of Wealth, (Business Plus, Hachette Book Group, New York City, NY, © 2009)*, W. Randall Jones interviewed LeRoy Landhuis. Landhuis said, "If you want to give your money away when you're dead, that's fine, but that doesn't mean anything to God, because He's got enough money. If you'll give it away while you're living, He gives you credit for that forever. If you don't believe in Him, you won't do it, though, because you won't do what you can't see or believe. It's too illogical for your human mind to grasp. You won't give away millions of dollars to change the lives of others unless you have real faith in God."

I can't understand why anyone would spend their lives accumulating wealth and not distribute it while they are living. The Bible is very clear that giving is a blessing. **If you want to experience real joy, then live to give.**

God has an established system of rewarding the giver.

Let me address a fallacy. It is a false belief system that has robbed so many men of the joy of giving. The man cloaked in false humility states, "I don't give to get. I expect nothing in return."

That's foolishness. Think about it. No one in his right mind does that. God certainly doesn't. When God gave His only begotten Son, He expected to reap sons. What farmer goes to the trouble of preparing ground and planting seed and doesn't expect a harvest?

The problem with that kind of thinking is that it's actually a spirit of pride. The Bible states that the lesser is blessed by the greater (Hebrews 7). So, the person who says, "I don't give to get" is actually saying, "I am in the superior position and I am giving to God." They're exalting themselves above God! They're hypocrites!

"GOD IS A CAPITALIST."
—LEROY LANDHUIS

A Fivestarman understands that he uses his entrepreneurial drive to gain the resources, influence, and finances in his life to meet his needs, to provide for his family, and even to leave them an inheritance, but he has also accumulated enough to leave the world a better place because he has lived.

The philanthropic cause within you may drive you to help a widow weatherize her home for the winter. Other men may join efforts to build a home for Habitat for Humanity. We have Fivestarmen who invest in sponsoring children through educational and humanitarian relief organizations.

Donating your time and effort is as simple as seeing a need and meeting it.

Think about how men are motivated. Men dream of changing the world. Against all odds, men are motivated to look back upon their lives with a congratulatory pat on the back, saying, "You did it."

That's it! There is a deep, driven, vibrant, even vehement current of activity within a man to be heroic in changing this world.

You see this demonstrated perfectly in the movie, *Braveheart,* when William Wallace says, "Aye, fight and you may die. Run and you'll live—at least a while. And dying in your beds many years from now, would you be willing to trade all the days from this day to that for one chance, just one chance to come back here and tell our enemies that they may take our lives, but they'll never take . . . our freedom!"

Don't surrender your talents, your abilities, or your creativity to simply retire to a golf course or fishing hole. Re-ignite your passion to leave a legacy.

LIVE WHILE YOU ARE LIVING

We sat down on the swing in the manicured back yard, near the shop where he refinished furniture and crafted his woodwork, a hobby that he enjoyed. Next to the shop was a garage with his bass boat. He had worked the grueling labor of shift work his whole life. My father-in-law sat down and talked to me man to man, in a way he never had before.

I was no longer the naïve young man who married his daughter. I was a man who was managing my own household and building my career. He was dying. Cancer had robbed him of his hair and reduced his thick body to a slimmer, sickly frame.

He looked across the yard, pondering his life. He spoke softly, "Neil, live while you are living." He paused and then sighed out his regret, "I've worked all my life to retire. Now that I can, I am dying. . . . What a waste."

I changed my thinking that day. I decided that I would go for it, to live the adventure, not to just coast through the ranks. I decided that I would believe God for bigger things. It motivated me to step out and risk it all.

Don't believe the lie. Don't pattern your life after the herd. Don't work and labor in vanity. Decide that you are going to live for significance. Find a cause that is worthy of your pursuit.

When men discover their cause it breathes new passion into their lives.

I'm intrigued by T. Boone Pickens, the Oklahoma energy tycoon. I identify with him because he grew up in a town that my team and I played high school football against, the town of Seminole. Even though Mr. Pickens is well past the age when most men sit down on their assets and drift off to sleep, he has created a campaign that is forcing the debate on our use of energy in America.

After amassing an enormous amount of wealth, Boone has dedicated himself to two primary endeavors: First, to convert the United States into making better use of our own resources, the incredible reserves that we have in natural gas; the second to make Oklahoma State University a leader in academics and a winner in national championships on the football field.

★ ★ ★ ★ ★

STEP UP YOUR GAME

As believers, we should not just believe that we can make a difference in the lives of a widow or an orphan, but **we should look at the world and say, "Why not?"**

Most men are not motivated by fame, that's more of an effeminate quality that's driven by narcissism. Authentic men want significance. They want to do something in their brief time on Earth that makes an impact.

Modern Christianity has replaced the adventurous, global impacting, risk taking, sacrificial faith of Christ and converted it into a weak, anemic, pacifist, tolerant, religion of appeasement. That kind of religion doesn't understand Jesus' statement, *"The kingdom of heaven forcefully advances"* (Matthew 11:12, author's paraphrase).

You were born for significance. You were uniquely gifted not only to make a living, not only to impact your family, but also to change the world in some way. I believe that.

> *"Now faith is being sure of what we hope for and certain of what we do not see. This is what the ancients were commended for. By faith we understand that the universe was formed at God's command, so that what is seen was not made out of what was visible" (Hebrews 11:1–3).*

The eleventh chapter of Hebrews is often called the "Hall of Faith." Those listed in the exclusive club did remarkable things that required faith, a belief that they were personally selected by God to impact the world.

If you read verse three, *"By faith we understand that the universe was formed at God's command, so that what is seen was not made out of what was visible,"* then you may conclude that it requires faith to believe in creation. It may for some. I believe the evidence overwhelmingly supports that the universe is not an accident, that some "bang" simply happened. I believe that God said, *"Let there be light,"* and bang it was so.

If you look closely at this verse, you'll see something interesting that will help you become motivated to do something of significance. What were those historical figures, who impacted their time and are still being talked about, commended or credited for? They were credited for what it says in verse three.

The word *universe* is *aion* in the Greek, which means *generation*. The word *formed* means to *change, shape, fashion, or mold*. The phrase *God's command* means *speaking revelation*.

Here's the point. The list of those mentioned in the "Hall of Faith," were commended for exercising faith *by speaking revelation that changed their generation!*

Apply that to your own life. **Is it possible that if you believed God for significance you could change your world?**

I believe so. I've seen remarkable things happen in the lives of men. I've seen men stand up tall, put their shoulders back, and believe to do something that requires more than they have within themselves, something that requires that they must believe God.

There is so much more to life than chasing after cars, clothes, and cottages. Don't lose your dignity by pursuing the young, vacuous-minded blonde. Don't embarrass yourself by drinking yourself into an imbecile. Invest your life in something that matters!

GET STARTED!

As you begin to allow the expression of the philanthropic cause to work in you, you will find that it becomes easier to give and to yield to the things God is calling you to do. There are a few things you need to remember along the way.

START SMALL.
Don't think that you have to give a million dollars to make a difference. I recommend that you first clean your closet. Go through your clothes and find what you haven't worn in three months. I like to make sure that my clothes are clean and folded before I drop them off at a reputable charity.

LOOK LOCALLY.

Find a need that your particular skill set can meet. For an example, if the city has a park that needs to be fixed up, recruit some men and spend a few hours on a Saturday sprucing up the park.

ASK YOUR PASTOR.

See if your church has a widow who needs some work done on her house. Get a few guys to go to her house and knock out the list of fix ups that she needs.

CONNECT WITH PARTNERS.

See if Habitat for Humanity is building a home in your city and partner with them.

DONATE YOUR TIME.

If you're a professional, give some of your time and skills to the poor.

Don't try to take on too much at first. Let your zeal for change process through the filter of wisdom. Too many men start out with a lot of fire, but they burn out quickly. Gradually work your way up to giving. You will discover many things that you need to know and be aware of in the process.

TIPS FOR GIVING:

KNOW THE RECIPIENT.

You would never invest in a stock if you don't know anything about the company. Learn what you can about the charity. Investigate their reputation in the community or through charity watch organizations. Find out about their rating and management.

WHERE WILL YOUR MONEY GO?

Look at their finances. I would not give to a charity that spends more than 25 percent on administration and fund-raising.

DON'T MAKE HASTE.

If the charity is pressured to get their money, they are making mistakes. If they're always facing emergencies and appealing for bailouts, there is something wrong. Discern their appeals. Don't give out of compulsion. You'll regret it.

DON'T GIVE SIMPLY BECAUSE YOU ARE FAMILIAR WITH THEIR NAME.

There are some very large organizations that receive millions in donations that are very poor stewards of their funds.

RE-EVALUATE YOUR GIVING AFTER A SEASON OF TIME.

Make certain that you're keeping a relationship with the charity.

SET GOALS FOR YOUR GIVING.

A Fivestarman entrepreneur told me, "Neil, I don't have income goals, I have giving goals."

DON'T DO IT FOR THE TROPHY.

We're motivated by God's approval, not man's acknowledgment. Sometimes the best place to give is the place that doesn't get a lot of attention.

MAKE SURE THAT YOU INVEST IN CHILDREN.
God has a supernatural response when we give to the
needs of children. My wife, Kay, and I invest in children
every month, and have for years. I know that God has
favored my children because of the financial giving that
we've done on their behalf.

As you develop the philanthropic gift within you, you will tap into
an energy that very few experience. A new wave of creativity and
excitement will become a part of your life. When you walk through
a crowd you'll sense a destiny in your steps. You'll look at your age
as nothing more than the passing of time, rather than counting the
days to your death.

LEGACY

The authentic man is designed to leave the world better than he
found it. My friend Tim Simmons spoke to this when he wrote the
lyrics of *"Legacy"* the anthem of Fivestarman, which I've included
on the following page.

LEGACY

by Tim Simmons

I will stand up and say
My King is the one true way
And I will gladly sign my name
Only to Him
If I bend, I won't break
Or bring shame to Your sweet name
My children will call You great
And bring to You glorious fame

And time will tell of my love for You, my King
And time will tell of my life and what I believe

I want to leave a legacy for those who will follow me
A godly inheritance for those who will bear my name
For when I leave time behind and stories are told of me
More than the good ol' times, I pray it's a legacy

I'll speak truth in spite of pain
And weep for the unborn babe
And when nations plot in vain I will stand up
I walk in my destiny, my eye fixed on purity
For those who are watching me, I will stay strong

When I spend my last days
Holding the ones I've raised
My gracious King will say,
Good job, well done.

I will lay at His feet the life He's given me
And I gladly say to Him, "Here is my legacy."

CONCLUSION

THE CHALLENGE

PROLOGUE

Ryan and Buddy were inseparable. Everywhere trouble was mentioned in the small city of Mount Pleasant, Ryan and Buddy were there. The townsfolk had a love/hate relationship with the two boys. Daily the town elders sat in the local diner, sipping their coffee and complaining how the hoodlums were nothing but trouble. Almost always, the stories started out with an angry tone, but as the tales unfolded, the diner crowd usually burst into laughter and secret wishes that they were young enough to join in the adventures. The mischief of Ryan and Buddy was so legendary that the locals blamed things on them years after they both had moved away.

When Ryan returned to Mount Pleasant, he couldn't believe how much the town had changed. Driving down Main Street, his mind was overtaken with a feeling of nostalgia. The buildings seemed to be smaller now. The large estate homes that lined the streets with their manicured lawns now showed signs of disrepair. It was surreal. As he reflected upon his childhood, joy and bitterness mixed in his emotions like a cocktail. Joy flooded him as he remembered his adventures with Buddy. He chewed on bitter morsels as he remembered the pain of his childhood home.

"What happened to my dreams?" Ryan muttered out loud. "I was so naïve. I thought that I could take on the world. Now look at me."

Ryan paused as he pulled into the driveway. Memories of his childhood raced through his head like an instant replay.

He pulled forward to park, took a deep breath, and put on his game face. As he walked to the door, he heard a voice so familiar that it immediately made him smile.

"Look out!" Buddy yelled as a football came crashing into Ryan's chest. It was a perfect hit right to the lungs that made Ryan gasp for breath. The first few minutes were a whirlwind, as the two old friends caught up on small talk and chatted about the town that they once had conquered.

But then the conversation waned. The bright smiles gave way to the gravitational pull of experience. The small talk was over. Soon they would dive into reality. Ryan knew that he would have to talk about it, but he hated the thought of it.

After a day of reflection on their childhood stunts, a visit to the coffee shop where the old men used to gather, and a drive past the high school football field, the duo returned to Buddy's childhood home. They sat down on the back porch. It was time.

Ryan dove into the story of how he had started out strong, but the years had worn him down. After pouring out the details, he concluded with this editorial, "I thought the energy and excitement we had as young men would do it. I thought I would win. The daily grind became so boring—so frustrating. It was everything I could do to just pay the bills. I'm in debt up to and beyond the limit. I lost my job. I thought they couldn't survive without me. Turns out it was pretty easy for them to let me go. And now—well, I'm about to lose my wife and children." The tears finally gushed out.

The moment was intimate and inappropriate at the same time. Ryan's vulnerability was so exposed that it was embarrassing.

Buddy reached out his hand, clenched it into a firm grip, and pulled Ryan into a man hug—a pat on the back confirmed the acknowledgement. "Ryan, let me tell you something. We're going to get through this. You can do it, and I'm going to help you."

Buddy invited Ryan to attend a small gathering of guys to talk. "It's called Fivestarman," Buddy explained. "We get together to talk about being real men—you know, the kind of guys that we all dreamed about being when we were young. But now we have strategies. You'll like it."

"Come on, I don't have time for a support group," Ryan objected. "I know I opened up to you tonight, but I'm not going to some confessional where a bunch of guys sit around and complain about their lives."

It took some convincing, but it finally worked. The next day when Buddy and Ryan drove into the parking lot, Ryan laughed out loud. "Church?! Are you kidding me?"

As they walked into the lobby, they greeted a dozen other men who were there. Most of them were average, but there were a few really sharp guys. Ryan could tell that they were focused, energetic, fit, and confident. He wanted that feeling. He put on his game face as Buddy introduced him. He didn't want to expose the embarrassment that had surfaced the day before.

After the introductions, Mike, a man's-man type of guy stepped up to take the lead. "Guys, we're ready to start The Challenge. Some of you have been through it before—others, this will be your first time, so let me go over the basics." As Mike shared The Challenge, the men listened as if they were a football team about to leave the locker room for the field. It was motivating.

Although he was still skeptical, Ryan sensed excitement and hope in his spirit. He recognized that what he was hearing was more than a mental exercise. It was resonating with something deep within him. It was gut level. It moved him.

Ryan looked at Buddy and asked, "Have you done this before?"

With a smile and a nod, Buddy replied, "Yep, it changed my life."

Without hesitation, Ryan picked up his copy of the Field Guide. The anticipation was palpable. He couldn't wait to start reading. "Day One, The Field of Contest." As he read through the chapter, it seemed too easy. "This will be a piece of cake." Ryan thought to himself.

Buddy saw the look on Ryan's face. He knew his friend well. "Ryan, don't underestimate this challenge. This will draw upon deep qualities that challenge your manhood. You may think you're a man, but this will require something beyond acting or 'gaming it.' This'll reach within the core of who you are."

Ryan found out soon enough that Buddy's words were true.

When Ryan left Mount Pleasant to return home, he wondered if things could be different. When he drove into the driveway, he mused about how he would tell his wife about The Challenge. He didn't want Candace thinking that this was just another fantasy or that he had somehow "found religion." He thought that he should tell her over dinner.

It took some convincing but Ryan persuaded Candace to meet him. He made the arrangements for the children to stay at her mother's, and he made reservations at their favorite restaurant, Ruth's Chris. Earlier in his career, Ryan would celebrate his victories with Candace over their amazing food, but it had been years since he felt the excitement of hope. Now, although he felt enthusiastic, he was very careful to temper it. He knew that he had forfeited his credibility with his wife. She would no longer just coast along with him through life.

"I need forty-five days," Ryan stated. "I'm requesting that we put everything on hold for forty-five days—the divorce, the bankruptcy, everything. . . just let me have forty-five days."

As Candace listened to Ryan, she wanted to believe him. Something was different in his tone. She saw a level of sincerity and resolve that she hadn't seen in years. She wanted him to reach out and grab her up into his arms. She wanted the comfort and the confidence from her husband that she used to know, but she sat there in doubt. "Do you really think that you can turn this mess around in forty-five days? Why should I try? Why should I play games with you anymore?"

Even though he didn't have a job, Ryan committed himself to get up early in the mornings as if he did. He read the first day of The Challenge again. He drove to where he had remembered seeing some guys coming out of the local high school. He discovered that they were working out to P90X together. They welcomed him in and got to work. It had been a long time. His muscles were resisting the effort, but the adrenaline started flowing as he pushed himself to finish the workout.

Day two, "Ignite Your Engine," made him dig deep. He realized that he needed some help. He went to the Strength Finders website and took the test. He usually despised personality tests. The ones that his company pushed always seemed to do more harm than good by causing doubt and confusion in the employees. Strength Finders was different, it exposed something about his natural gifting that he hadn't realized before. He discovered that he wanted to be strong in areas that he wasn't. He realized that he had been faking it all along.

"No wonder I was bored and frustrated with my work. I was a pretender."

After seeing the list of his strengths, he began to make a list of possible jobs he could do. Then he thought, "I believe that I can do this—I really believe that this is what I can accomplish. It will take some time to gather the resources, but this can turn into something lucrative."

The days began to fly by. It was amazing to see the steps that he was taking. Each day of The Challenge he began to see incremental progress in his life. Candace saw it too. She hadn't fully come around, but she was starting to laugh again.

As was his new custom, Ryan got up early, read the day's challenge, and found a place to pull over into the woods. He started walking. The trail became a temple. For the first time in a long time, Ryan prayed. He didn't attempt to be religious. He knew that he couldn't fake it; he wanted to have a real dialogue with God.

"God, I know that I need You in my life. I realize what a poser I am. I never understood that You really wanted a relationship with me personally. I also didn't know that Jesus was a real man—a man's man—I can't imagine what kind of man could endure the agony of His sacrifice. He wasn't an appeaser, a tolerant, effeminate pretty boy—no, Jesus was a bold man with a bold plan to change my life by defeating the things that I couldn't beat on my own." Ryan's words were so real and affirming that he knew God was walking with him. That day, Ryan became a man, authentic in his relationship with his Creator.

The daily challenges forced him to confront uncomfortable things in his life. He could no longer push them under the rug. He couldn't avoid the phone calls from bill collectors. He began to relate to his children on a level that he never had before. They ran to him, rather than from him. Candace began to change. After she had seen Ryan go through his closet donating more than half of his clothes to charity, she began to dress differently. Her makeup seemed not to cover her face anymore, but to compliment her natural beauty. Not to mention her eyes—those eyes that first caught Ryan's attention as young love does—her eyes suddenly began to sparkle again.

Ryan received encouragement from his lifelong friend, Buddy, and also from the Fivestarman website. The Challenge drew something out of him everyday. It wasn't making him become something he wasn't, but it was revealing someone that he was already. It simply made him become a better man.

The forty-five days were almost over. So much had changed that Ryan barely recognized himself when he walked by a mirror. "How could so much change in just a few days?" he asked himself.

Buddy and Ryan meet again in Mount Pleasant. As they sat down in the church lobby, Ryan was different. He had changed physically from the workouts. His clothes were a much better representation of who he was and where he wanted to go in life. When he introduced himself to other men, he no longer put on his game face, but with confidence, he looked them in the eye and affirmed them. When Mike started the Engage Huddle, he said, "Guys, it's been an amazing time. So much has happened. I'd like to congratulate you on succeeding in The Challenge."

Ryan looked at Buddy, "This has changed my life. I'm just getting started on becoming the man that God originally intended for me to be. Thanks for being a real friend. Thanks for helping me get out of my comfort zone and step up to The Challenge."

THE CHALLENGE

When I entered the ninth grade, I was a really small boy. I wrestled for the high school team at 108 pounds. I also played football, but I rarely started because of my small frame. I asked my brother, who was an outstanding football player, to help me develop my skills. He laughed, "Sure, get your motorcycle helmet." After I put it on, he instructed me to run at him and tackle him. I ran at him full blast.

When I got near him he threw his forearm across my head, spinning the helmet completely around. After I got up to shake it off, I felt a ringing in my head. I was dizzy, shaken. He said, "Come on, do it again." Foolishly I repeated the attempt over and over until I had a massive headache. He laughed at me. Mocked me. Ridiculed me. I became angry. Something deep within me kept rising up to challenge him again and again.

The first day of football practice I went to the field determined. Even though I was one of the smallest guys on the team, I worked hard. During practice, Coach Combs called us to form a "bullring," basically a training exercise when one lone player stands in the middle of the pack to be creamed by the other players. I watched as player after player stood waiting their turn to be tormented. Then it was my turn. Coach Combs said, "Neil, get out there."

When I stood in the middle of the players, my eyes fixed on their numbers. When Coach yelled out their numbers, I instinctively ran to them knocking them down before they had time to figure out that their number had been called. Over and over, Coach called out a number. Over and over, I ran at each one of them, turning the tables on the exercise.

My brother trained me to go after the fight. Because of the challenge, I became a starter on the freshman team that went undefeated that year.

All men need a challenge.

THE FIVESTARMAN FIELD GUIDE AND 45-DAY CHALLENGE

Fivestarman has a challenge for you. We have developed the *Fivestarman Field Guide and 45-Day Challenge* as your opportunity to embrace and process the Five Passions of Authentic Manhood into your life.

Each day, you will be challenged to exercise a passion that will make you a stronger man. The challenges will motivate a passion that will draw upon the deep waters of your purpose. As you incorporate these challenges you will discover new conditioning in your body, new ideas will arise in your mind, passion will be rekindled in your marriage or relationships, new causes to pursue will present themselves, and new business ideas will begin to develop. You will also develop a new walk in your faith.

Along the way, we will support you online at www.Fivestarman. com with ideas and insights as to how other men have accomplished the tasks. Some of the challenges will be easy, while others will require a real commitment and discipline to accomplish.

As you go through the 45-Day Challenge we recommend that you huddle with other men at a Fivestarman Engage.

This small-group setting will help motivate you and surround you with an atmosphere of camaraderie.

The Fivestarman Field Guide and 45-Day Challenge will kick start your day as you continually work through resurrecting authentic manhood in your life. You'll shake off those things that hinder you and press toward the mark of the higher calling in your life.

So, man up and start the challenge!

THE FIVESTARMAN INITIATIVE

Fivestarman exists to inspire, instruct, and empower men to live the authentic and passionate life that God intended. But we are not called to go it alone.

We believe a man cannot fully live the authentic life to which he is called without a close walk with his Creator and the camaraderie of his fellow man. The Initiative seeks to enlist hundreds of churches, men's groups, business organizations and more to participate in the Fivestarman Initiative by launching a local chapter of Fivestarman.

To be clear, the Fivestarman Initiative is **NOT** a program or a men's ministry—it is designed to be a movement of authentic men led by strong and equipped men. Our strategy is built upon the biblical pattern of men serving as the gateway to the entire family.

In the book, *Why Men Hate Going to Church,* David Murrow said, "When a mother comes to faith in Christ, the rest of her family follows 17 percent of the time. But when a father comes to faith in Christ, the rest of the family follows 93 percent of the time."

The Initiative is a simple, biblical model that draws upon the five passions that every man has deep within him. The goal is not to place a man under a heavy load of guilt or condemnation, but rather to draw out the inner gifts God has placed within, thereby harmonizing his inner man with authentic manhood.

THE STRATEGY

Fivestarman has developed a proven strategy to help you realize your dream of reaching the men in your community. We've found that this strategy is easy to implement because it provides a more organic approach than a typical men's program or ministry effort. It draws upon the deep purposes and passions of a man that he wants to express.

The Fivestarman Initiative expresses the five passions of authentic manhood through:

FIVESTARMAN EXCURSIONS

The Adventurous Spirit is expressed through Excursions. A Fivestarman Excursion is when men get together and go onto the field of contest—that can be a football field, baseball field, or even a battlefield. Any time men get together to face a challenge, they draw upon the Adventurous Spirit.

What is truly amazing about the field of contest is that it draws upon the spiritual side of man. It encourages his deep need for risk and reward. It challenges his sense of contest. It inspires him to be conditioned, not only physically, but also spiritually. When men are engaged in a contest they often begin to converse about deeper things in their lives. It doesn't have to be programmed. It's simply a natural expression of the adventurous spirit.

FIVESTARMAN ENTERPRISE

The Entrepreneurial Drive is expressed through Fivestarman Enterprise. It is the marketplace expression of Fivestarman. It's an opportunity to network with businessmen and draw upon each other's strengths to become better in business and more strategic in success.

Business luncheons, seminars, simulcasts, and small group meetings give the Fivestarman information and develop relationships that mutually benefit those attending.

We're seeing hundreds of men discover their unique gifts and launch new businesses. They embrace the risk for the joy that is set before them—the reward! We all need to sharpen our skills and learn new strategies, so the networking provided through Fivestarman Enterprise is vital.

FIVESTARMAN ENGAGE

Fivestarman Engage is like a huddle where a small group of men gather to plan and strategize their next moves to become better at whatever topic they find interesting, such as faith studies, investment strategies, marriage enrichment, etc. Again, these are more organic than programmed. It is amazing how when a few guys get together they sharpen one another.

FIVESTARMAN ENCOUNTER

A very important strategy for Fivestarman is the Encounter. An Encounter is a gender-exclusive meeting that is carefully designed to communicate to men. It's also a great time to invite men who have given up on the church ever relating to them as men.

The Encounter is an exciting atmosphere of faith. It's a spiritual rally without being religious, where carefully selected speakers communicate on a variety of practical and spiritual matters.

FIVESTARMAN EXPLOITS

To express the Philanthropic Cause of the Fivestarman, we recommend that men use their gifts to better mankind. Fivestarman Exploits, such as mission trips, building homes for Habitat for Humanity, feeding families on the holidays, weatherizing widows' homes, etc., are all activities that motivate men to look outside of themselves and unto others.

FIVESTARMAN.COM
THE VOICE OF AUTHENTIC MANHOOD

We've designed and continue to update the Fivestarman. com website, which is the Voice of Authentic Manhood. This site is designed for men. The articles communicate the truths of our five passions and aggregate information that men find of interest. The website also serves as our central voice to communicate with Fivestarman Initiatives.

FIVESTARMAN FIELD GUIDES

The Fivestarman Field Guide and 45-Day Challenge serves as the companion to the book, *Fivestarman—The Five Passions of Authentic Manhood.* The handy, pocket-sized Field Guide will challenge you to incorporate the five passions of authentic manhood into your life and give you daily strategies to revive the passions within you. More information can be found at Fivestarman.com for each of the daily challenges.

CENTURIONS—LEADERS OF MEN

The word *authority* causes many people to cringe. And it's true that authority is often used for self-promotion and control. But *Centurion Principle* is based on the authority that Jesus taught: servant leadership. It digs deep into the practical principles that equip a man to understand that authority exists in his life to empower, protect, promote, and prosper those who are part of his world. Based soundly on the biblical concept of godly authority, *Centurion Principle* gives men the ability to walk with the dignity of manhood and the controlled meekness of true leaders. This valuable resource helps men understand how authority flows through leadership, not around it.

THE COST

Here's the amazing part. Registering to participate in the Fivestarman Initiative is absolutely FREE. We have strived to remove all barriers to any group, no matter how small or large, to participate in the Initiative.

Your participation enables you to launch a local chapter of Fivestarman and provides you full access to the branding, strategies, tools, resources, videos, and training programs that Fivestarman has developed and will continue to develop.

There is, of course, the cost of your time and efforts. To embrace your role as a Centurion, a leader of men, you will undoubtably encounter additional constraints on your time and resources, and this role is not for the faint of heart. But consider this: If you launch a local chapter of Fivestarman and begin to communicate the five passions and give them expression using the designed strategy you will see more men come to know Christ than ever before.

You will instruct, inspire, and empower men to resurrect authentic manhood and that is truly a worthwhile and lasting legacy.

JOIN THE INITIATIVE

If you feel the call to help in our quest to challenge and encourage men and would like to start your own Fivestarman group, visit us at Fivestarman.com and join the Fivestarman Initiative today.

ABOUT THE AUTHOR

Neil Kennedy has passionately promoted God's Word for twenty-five plus years of ministry. He is known for practically applying biblical principles that elevate people to a new level of living. As a business, church, ministry, and life consultant, Neil has helped others strategize the necessary steps to reach their full potential.

In 2008, Neil founded Fivestarman. His full time focus is now on Fivestarman and he travels extensively each week speaking in churches and seminars challenging men to step up and grab the reins of authentic manhood. Neil and his wife, Kay, have three children and reside in the Gulf Bay area of Fairhope, Alabama.

MORE RESOURCES

In addition to *Fivestarman — The Five Passions of Authentic Manhood*, Neil has also authored:

- *The 7 Laws Which Govern Increase and Order*
- *God's Currency*
- *Centurion Principle — The Protocol of Authority*

CONTACT US

To contact the author or to obtain information on Fivestarman events,

Please Contact:
Neil Kennedy / Fivestarman
82 Plantation Pointe
Fairhope, AL 36532
Fivestarman.com

Prayer requests are welcome.

RESURRECTION OF
AUTHENTIC MANHOOD

Gathering the dry land
The Creator cloned the Man

Sculpted in His image
Inherent to the message

Ingredients of Earth and Divine
Man committed the original crime

Allowing the serpent to speak to his wife
The man forfeited eternal life

A second Man entered the Earth
To give manhood the new birth

Born of water out of the womb
Born of spirit out of the tomb

Courageous on the field of contest
The Man proved his ultimate best

Out of His belly flow deep rivers
Which cause the nemesis to shiver

Authentic manhood without concession
Will have its day of resurrection

—Neil Kennedy

To order your copy of the
Fivestarman Field Guide and 45-Day Challenge
please visit www.myhealthychurch.com.

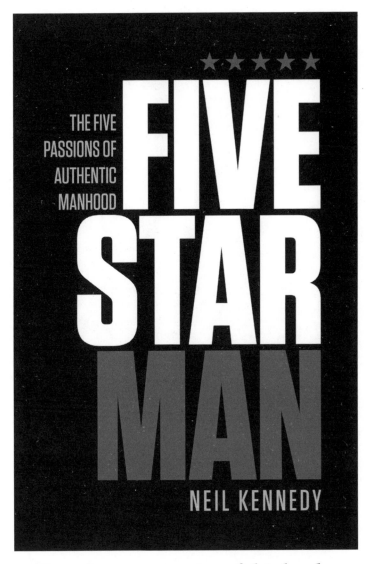

To order more copies of this book
visit www.myhealthychurch.com

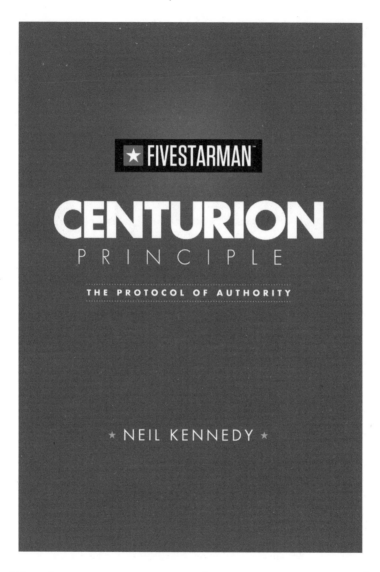